# UNCONDITIONAL LOVE

## A TRUE LOVE STORY

KAREN SACCHETTI

XULON PRESS ELITE

Xulon Press Elite
2301 Lucien Way #415
Maitland, FL 32751
407.339.4217
www.xulonpress.com

Printed in the United States of America.

ISBN-13: 978-1-5456-4542-0

# *table of Contents*

# 1

## Arrival in Paradise

❦

**JUNE 2010**

"Aloha. I needed to hear the sound of your voice, Karen. You could read me the dictionary all night long. That's how much I love the sound of your voice," Peter said in his charming, deep voice. Minutes before he called, I had been eagerly waiting to hear from him.

"Listen to this, Karen," Peter said as he put me on his speakerphone. It wasn't a song that I recognized. He was playing his harmonica over the phone for me. I started laughing, and he did too. "You laugh like a little billy goat," he said. I laughed back as I sank deeply into the plush maroon pillows on the off-white sofa. It wasn't the first time he had teased me. This was our private joke.

I reached for my laptop and pulled up my favorite picture of Peter. In the photo he is coming out of his pool. His black hair is slicked back, and his demeanor is aristocratic. "Stop your giggling, Karen," Peter said in a serious tone. "I need to talk to you straight from my heart."

I had calmed down from laughing. There was no question that Peter had swept me off my feet.

"I'm certain that you are the one, Karen. You have the combination of heart and beauty that I've always sought in a woman. I love you; I want you to be my wife. I want you here."

*Can this be real?* I asked myself. I had to pinch myself, shocked that Peter had asked me to spend my life with him as his wife.

"You've just made me the happiest woman in the world," I said. "Yes, I want to marry you."

"I love you. Let's get married right away," Peter responded.

We had spent only four months getting acquainted over the phone in a long-distance relationship, and our love had blossomed. I longed to be in a loving and intimate relationship. We had invested many hours in getting to know each other. Peter and I had met through an online dating site where he had found me, initiating contact first through e-mail.

I'll never forget the first time we spoke on the phone. The intense chemistry was evident throughout our conversation, which lasted for hours and hours. I loved the sound of his distinctive voice, his energy, and his intellect, and found him totally fascinating. Not only was he highly perceptive on a genius level, but he was a true "original" in every sense of the word. We also loved having fun, and he joked around and entertained me over the phone. However, we were challenged with living so far apart: I lived in southern Rhode Island, and Peter lived in southern Florida.

Because I knew I was in love and attracted to this charming, intelligent man, I needed confirmation of his sincerity. I tested Peter. If he was truly sincere about me being the one, his bride-to-be, I decided he would have to declare his intentions to my parents as well.

"I can't wait to share the news with my parents. Let's call them," I said. "First, my father."

"Okay," he said. "I need a cocktail first." I understood that he was nervous about asking my father for my hand in marriage. I held Peter accountable.

"What is your dad's number?" Peter asked. "We'll have to make a three-way call."

I was certain that my parents would be skeptical. And they were when we called them.

My dad responded, "Well, if you two are sure of this, it is quite a commitment that you are making. I wish you nothing but the best."

Next, we called my mother in Pennsylvania. "Hi, Mom. I have Peter on the phone with me. We have some news that we would like to share with you." I was nervous and anxious about what she would say about Peter's marriage proposal.

She hesitated before responding. There were no congratulatory comments. It was actually an awkward conversation.

"Have you two really thought this through?" she asked. "But you two haven't spent enough time together. Have you set the date?" I heard the anxiety and concern in her voice as a protective mother.

"No, we haven't set any date," I replied.

After we got off the phone with my parents, we talked about our future plans. "I'm buying you a baby grand piano as a wedding gift," Peter proclaimed. He expressed his interest in filling the house with music since he knew I enjoyed playing the piano. I had been passionate about music and dance since I was eight years old, when I took my first piano and ballet lessons.

As crazy as this marriage proposal seemed, I regarded myself as a risk-taker whose heart stirred over this man. I also knew God hadn't created me to live a safe, comfortable, mediocre life. God didn't create me just to have a job and a paycheck. He created me for a purpose, a cause larger than myself. I had always lived passionately and adventurously, taking steps of faith for what I believed.

Although I had never been married, I believe marriage is a higher institution of not only commitment, but of sacrifice to a higher cause beyond the self. Marriage should never be a convenient way of coming together to have one's selfish needs met. Marriage needs to be based on love and sacrifice.

I had decided I wanted to live on the east coast of South Florida long before Peter found me. It seemed magical, like it was all meant to be. I had already envisioned moving to Florida, and now along came "Prince Charming," who had swept me off my feet. I floated sky high on a cloud, excited about the new future that awaited me in sunny Florida.

Before meeting Peter, I was successfully self-employed for twelve years as a creative-dance educator. I taught in schools in addition to having my own studio in the church where I was a member. I had also sung and performed in four musical theater productions in Boston and southern Rhode Island before teaching dance.

When the economy tanked in the 2008 recession, like a domino effect, I lost all of my accounts in the schools and my business took a nosedive. It devastated me to witness all that I had worked for being torn from me. I felt God speaking through my intuition that it was time to leave Rhode Island and start anew. Interestingly enough, Rhode Island's greatest exodus of residents leaving the state occurred from April 2010 to July 2013. My exodus from Rhode Island occurred during June 2010. In 2013, Rhode Island had the second-highest unemployment rate in the country. As of 2015, Rhode Island was in the bottom five worst states economically.

I also came to the realization that the man I had been dating for eight years in Rhode Island before meeting Peter would never allow us to progress further. David's fear of commitment, which stemmed from his past divorce, was a wound that he was unwilling to heal. Although he was a loving father and a romantic at heart, like me, I accepted that we would never be more. Additionally, the small coastal town where I lived in Rhode Island constantly reminded me of David. I couldn't escape him. I was ready for change and once again seeking love. Peter was the catalyst, the gateway into Florida. Peter found me and pursued me to no end.

I also felt it was the right move because my sister had lived in South Florida for more than fifteen years with her long-term boyfriend. Interestingly enough, she had never offered me a place to stay in her three-bedroom home. This arrangement would have been the more practical route for dating Peter and thus, assimilating into South Florida. However, who wants practicality when it comes to love?

When I informed my sister of my plans to move to South Florida, she was not as happy for me as I had thought she would be. I shared all the details of how Peter and I had met and fallen in love. Even though she may have been apprehensive about the unconventional way we had met, I thought she would at least be excited to learn that her sister, with whom she shared a close relationship, would be moving close to her. That was not the case. She tried to sound delighted about my news, but she was not. But with or without her approval, I eagerly anticipated this new chapter of my life.

I said goodbye to my friends and the memories of Rhode Island as I packed up my life. I headed toward my mother's home in central Pennsylvania with a rental truck filled with my possessions. I stored my belongings in a temporary storage unit near my mother's home. My mother and I spent thirty days having a lovely visit before I flew to my new home in the Sunshine State. With my move to the opposite end of the country, I knew that it would be a while until I saw my mother again. This opportunity gave me high-quality time to spend with my mother, more so than the typical yearly Christmas visits lasting a week.

Additionally, Heidi, a dear, old high school and college friend, lived near my mother in the town where we had gone to high school. I greatly enjoyed spending time with Heidi. I'll never forget us sipping our cocktails at her pool as we reminisced about old times. She also had a chance to speak to Peter, since he typically called me three or four times a day on my cell phone. He made her laugh with his charming comments and asked Heidi various questions about me. He desired to be close to me daily through the long-distance phone calls. This monthlong visit also gave me time to reflect about whether this move was right for me. I knew destiny was calling my name and there was no going back.

The day had arrived for my new life to begin in Florida. Before leaving for the airport, my perfectionism kicked in to look my best. I wore a beautiful, feminine pink shirt with blue jeans. I fixed my hair and makeup to look picture-perfect for my arrival in Florida. After all, my husband-to-be and I would be laying eyes on each other for the first time. My mother and her companion, Art, drove me to the airport in State College. Not only was this small airport close to her home, but it was also home to the Pennsylvania State University where I had gone to college for four years. After I boarded the plane, I felt excited and anxious. I couldn't wait to meet Peter. The dream of my new life awaited me.

Although I love flying and find traveling exciting, this was the worst flying experience I'd ever had. The plane ride was extremely turbulent because of unusually strong wind patterns, and we circled the Philadelphia airport several times before landing. My stomach was nauseated as the plane dropped suddenly in an up-and-down roller-coaster-like motion. I had never experienced anything quite as turbulent as that flight. Afraid and questioning in my mind if we would land safely, I prayed to God for protection and safety. Finally, we landed safely in Philadelphia. However, I missed my connecting flight to West Palm Beach.

Catching a later flight, I finally arrived at the West Palm Beach airport three hours later. I collected my three large pieces of luggage and went outside searching for Peter's driver, Sean. Sean found me and escorted me to the limousine Peter had arranged for me. He called Peter and notified him that he had me in the car and that we would arrive shortly. He drove me to my long-awaited husband-to-be. I felt a great deal of anticipation, like I could hardly take it anymore.

We were cleared to go through the security gate at the Encantada development where Peter lived. Although it was dark, I saw that the homes were architecturally beautiful, and lush flowers and palm trees lined the manicured street. My heart raced as I took a couple of deep breaths to calm myself down. I had arrived at Peter's palace in Boca Raton. It was midnight.

Peter and I laid eyes on each other for the first time. He looked dashing in his red shirt, with his broad shoulders and dark, slicked-back hair. He was exactly how I had imagined him to look in person. I felt like I was in a dream-like altered state. It all felt incredibly surreal. We had already known what each other looked like from photos. We had already known the sound of our voices. Now at last, we were finally together.

Although Peter had always sounded confident over the phone, he seemed rather taken back by our being together in person for the first time. I'm certain we both fought our insecurities in our longing to be accepted. I certainly wanted our relationship to work out, despite the unusual manner in which we had come together. We said very little in the beginning as we gazed deeply into each other's eyes. Our physical chemistry was powerful. We sat and talked briefly on his leather sofa, feeling very attracted and in love. I completely wanted to capture the moment as I floated into the fairy tale.

It had been a long day of traveling. It was late, and Peter suggested I get some rest. As we went to sleep in the master bedroom, the moonlight peered through the sliding glass door that led to the pool. He joked with me, "I'm salsa and you're spaghetti," because he is part Latino and I am part Italian. He lovingly said to me as he held me in his arms before we drifted off to sleep, "I am determined to do whatever it takes to make us work. Sleep well, my love."

# 2

## Getting to Know You, Getting to Know All About You

The next morning, Cindy arrived as she did every Thursday to water dozens of indoor plants and to pay Peter's bills, run errands for him, and so on. It was late in the morning when I changed into my blue bathing suit to lie by the pool. As I entered the lanai, I looked behind me and noticed that Peter and Cindy had gone into his office and that the glass doors were shut. This created an uncomfortable feeling inside me. *Why do they feel the need to talk behind closed doors and exclude me from the conversation?* I asked myself.

It was a warm, sunny morning in Florida, and I proceeded outside toward the pool behind the house and jumped in playfully, like a dolphin repeatedly diving into the water. I was filled with happiness in my new home with my husband-to-be. Later that afternoon,

Peter shared with me that it gave him great joy to see me enjoying myself that way in the pool.

Later that evening, we ordered Chinese food to be delivered. While we waited for dinner, I began to admire Peter's beautiful art collection. Peter had an eye for colorful, contemporary art with his Peter Max lithographs, Britto paintings, and Salvatore Principe collages. I was thrilled that Peter was not only intellectual, but appreciated fine art, as do I. I felt like a princess living in his palace. The unique, exterior Spanish architecture of his beautiful home combined with the interior cathedral ceilings to exude a grandiose feeling. Life seemed too good to be true.

After dinner was over, I asked Peter why he and Cindy had closed his office doors earlier. He explained to me that Cindy found me "too goody-goody" for his taste. Peter set the record straight by letting Cindy know that he liked and preferred that I was not into drugs or alcohol and that I had been a Sunday school teacher in Rhode Island. I certainly did my fair share of partying in high school and attended one of the largest party universities in the country. However, that party lifestyle was long over. Since giving my heart to Christ in my late thirties, I have tried to live a moral life. Although Peter was raised Catholic, and I found a Bible on the nightstand next to his bed, he was not an active follower of Christ.

Not only was I in love with Peter, but I loved the Florida lifestyle. The laid-back summer days blurred into weeks. Weeks had passed before I noticed that Peter had not left the house—not even once. Like him, I wasn't working. Peter had had a successful career as a stockbroker in addition to living off the inheritance he'd received after his father had passed away. I enjoyed being at home with him around the clock.

I gradually realized that his alcohol consumption was heavier than I had first observed as well. Once, while drunk, Peter said, "I love watching TV with you." We often watched comedy movies on his leather sofa with our legs intertwined like a grapevine. We seemed to always laugh at the same time. At times, Peter made me feel like I was the most beautiful woman in the world. No other man had ever made me feel so beautiful inside.

A few weeks later, I met a couple of Peter's friends. His friend Mark brought some friends over to have a few cocktails, and we threw a little party at the house. They invited us to come out with them later that evening, but we declined.

Weeks turned into months, but Peter had still not left the house other than a walk at night around the neighborhood when I insisted he get some exercise. I drew the only logical conclusion: Peter had become a recluse. He drank his Bacardi rum heavily, watched movies, napped, and talked continually on the phone. These activities formed his daily ritual. *But how could this be?* I asked myself. He appeared to be an accomplished man—a college-educated man; a former second-string punter for his college football team, the Georgia Bulldogs; a former stockbroker; and a triathlon athlete. *Gorgeous, successful, and intellectual. What's wrong with this picture?*

Peter typically rose around 6:00 in the morning, starting his day with a cocktail and a phone call to a woman named Lois, who appeared to be a phone buddy. He napped late in the morning and always insisted that I nap with him, even though I wasn't tired at 11:00 a.m. Then he napped again late in the afternoon around 4:00 p.m. Once when he woke up after a nap, he pinched my thigh in a teasing way. "Ouch! Why did you just pinch me so hard?" I demanded.

"Oh, stop being a little baby, Lovey," he replied. "Lovey" was his nickname for me.

I also became concerned about his health deteriorating, because he never ate anything of substance all day. The only food he seemed to crave was junk food, including ramen-noodle binges for a while. "What takes you so long to make a three-minute ramen-noodle dish?" he demanded.

"Peter, relax, it's coming. Where is thy patience?" I teased him.

Although steam was still rising from the bowl, he quickly took a bite of the noodles and then screamed, "This is too hot!" slamming the bowl down onto the coffee table. Clearly, he lacked patience at times.

His alcoholism escalated to the point that he began to scream at me on a regular basis. I suffered from his verbal lashings while he was under the influence. Occasionally I called and cried on the phone to my sister. From time to time I also heard Peter on the phone screaming at various individuals, particularly debt collectors. Even though it appeared on the surface that Peter lived a posh and affluent life, I sensed that he was slowly drowning in debt. I believe his financial debts—primarily not paying his mortgage—led to his drinking.

One day the lawn crew mowed the grass and trimmed the hedges. Peter had me go buy sandwiches for the crew for lunch, which was kind of him. As I was driving back with the sandwiches, he called me on my cell phone and yelled, "What the hell is taking you so long?"

"Peter, calm down. I'll be there as soon as I can. They are doing construction on Powerline Road, converging two lanes into one," I answered.

Peter called a few more times, provoking me with the same rhetoric that I was taking too long to bring home sandwiches for the workers. Tears flooded my eyes, even while I knew it was ridiculous. Being the sensitive woman that I am, I became acutely aware that I was living with a reclusive, raging alcoholic. As time went by, I realized that Peter could never give me the marriage and life I deserved.

Peter had many female friends with whom he talked regularly, some even daily. In the beginning, it didn't faze me, but as time went on, I noticed that he spent more time on his cell phone with his office doors shut than he spent with me. He loved having fun on the phone with these women and did a lot of joking around. Once I questioned him about the many women with whom he spent time on the phone. He quickly responded, "This relationship will never work if you question me regarding other women."

Based on his comment, I felt the need to protect myself, and I checked his cell phone out of curiosity while he napped one evening.

I was shocked and devastated by what I found. Not only did Peter converse with several women daily, but he told perhaps a dozen women that he loved and missed them. The text messages said he was on the golf course or out on the boat with his friend Mark when he actually never left the house. I had initially thought that because he was a recluse, all of his friendships with women were harmless. After all, he wasn't spending any time with them physically, only through the phone.

Being the detective that I am, I then checked a popular online dating site. I found that Peter had an active profile seeking love on that site while living with me. I know that at times I am naïve and too trusting of people, particularly men. I felt devastated when I learned that Peter had told these women that he loved them and that he had an active profile on a dating site. It all became too much for me to handle. This wasn't what I had signed up for. Peter was unable to give me 100 percent commitment. I knew that God wanted me to have a better life than the one I was living.

One afternoon, Peter handed me his house phone. "Here, say hello to Mike," he suggested. Mike was his younger brother and also lived in South Florida. Mike suggested that if I became bored, I should go shopping at the mall in Boca Raton. Later during the call, Mike said, "If you have any problems with Peter, call me." He then gave me his phone number. It was as if Mike already knew what I was experiencing with his brother. He displayed a sympathetic, caring quality, and I immediately felt a sense of comfort after speaking with him.

A month later, I overheard Peter in his home office with the glass doors shut, talking on the phone to a woman he no doubt had met online. His jovial question asking prompted me to press my ear closer to the wall so that I could hear a bit of what was going on.

Peter proceeded to ask her questions about her job, what grade she taught, and what she liked to do for fun. They were the kind of questions a man would ask when pursuing a woman. He had no idea that I was listening to his conversation like a spy. Nor did he catch on that I even knew about his online dating site; I had kept my discovery a secret.

Later he talked to his friend Mark, saying, "Yeah, I'm taking Karen to dinner for her birthday, but I'm not spending a lot of money on a dinner for her." By now, I was repulsed by Peter's womanizing. He made false promises to women, promising them, as he had me, marriage and a life together. All of the pieces came together like a puzzle. I no longer had any expectations of us moving forward as a couple.

I needed space to get my head together. The initial infatuation with Peter had blindsided me. I hadn't taken into account that we had different values and walked two different paths in terms of our beliefs. I was in my spiritual infancy in regard to my Christian walk in that I didn't have the cognizance to understand the importance of being united with a man who shared my faith.

Peter once admitted to me that he was "half heart, half heartless." He possessed many strengths and admirable qualities in spite of his lack of integrity with women. For example, he was interested in buying a children's Brazilian soccer academy. He asked me to type up a proposal while I was living with him. I truly believed he wanted to make a difference in the lives of those young boys, given his background in sports.

I tried to help Peter before my birthday dinner. After I had seen a TV commercial, I researched online and called one of the best alcohol recovery centers in Hawaii. I searched locally as well for different ways to help him overcome his alcoholism. Although he had hurt me with his behavior toward other women, I knew he suffered from deep depression and used alcohol to numb himself.

However, Peter, with his strong self-discipline, made the decision to quit drinking on his own two months after I had moved in with him. He never discussed his decision with me other than to say he needed a few days alone in the master bedroom to detox from the alcohol. Once he was sober, though, I saw a cold, mean-spirited side of Peter that I didn't like. On a Sunday afternoon, he lay by the pool with his boom box playing. I lay in the chaise next to him. He never even said two words to me. It was as if we were strangers at a resort pool with no verbal exchange. He had been more jovial and fun loving while drinking, even with his temperamental outbursts. It was as if I didn't know how to relate to the "sober" Peter. As reality came crashing through, I came to the conclusion that my being in love with Peter had been more of an infatuation.

The only time the reclusive Peter left his home was when he took me to dinner on my birthday to a Japanese buffet restaurant. The night out was actually the first time he had left his house in our two and a half months of living together. The server asked if we were brother and sister, because it was apparent that no real love connection emanated from us.

Peter loved to boast about how women stared at him whenever he walked down the street. The only time I was ever out in the world with him, I didn't see anybody checking him out. Oddly enough, with the uncertainty about Peter surrounding me, I shined more brightly that evening. It was my birthday. I wore a beautiful floral dress that he had paid for during the first month of my stay, when he entrusted me with his debit card. I felt like Queen Anne going to my final dinner before King Henry the Eighth ordered my beheading. Little did I know what lay ahead.

# 3

## *Rainbow in the Sky*

❧

**September 2010**

N ow sober, Peter informed me that he had to take a business trip to Texas for the weekend. "Hey, hon, since I have to go away, why don't you spend the weekend with your sister?" he suggested. He then added, "You should take all of your belongings with you."

I paused before responding reluctantly. "Okay, Peter, I'll call my sister now. I haven't spent much time with her lately. Let's see what she's up to this weekend." I found his comment about taking my belongings with me strange. I knew deep down we needed space from each other. I also felt intuitively that I would never be returning to live with him and that the weekend was going to be my exit out of this nightmare. Tossing and turning all night, I found that sleep eluded me because of all the unknowns lurking deep inside.

The next morning, I packed in preparation of leaving to go to my sister's home in Palm Beach Gardens, about forty-five minutes away. Peter arranged for a limousine driver to take me to her house, and we hugged goodbye. I didn't recognize this new driver; he was not Sean, who had driven me to Peter's house from the airport when I'd moved there months earlier. While on the highway, I asked the driver, "Has Peter booked a time for you to pick him up tomorrow for the airport?" Of course the driver answered, "No." I knew intuitively that Peter had lied. He was not traveling on business as he had said. The driver confirmed my suspicions. No doubt Peter planned to bring a woman into the house after I'd left.

After I slept overnight in my sister's guest bedroom, Peter called me first thing Saturday morning to make sure I was okay. He then said, "I think it is best if you continue to stay with your sister." I agreed that it was the best for both of us. Additionally, the manner in which he ended our relationship confirmed my intuition and my theory about why he had wanted me to take all of my suitcases. Peter behaved like a coward: he didn't have the courage to tell me directly in person that he wanted to end our relationship. He waited until I was at my sister's to tell me his decision. My presence in his home had obstructed his womanizing.

The fairy tale was over. I no longer felt in love with him, although I felt sadness creep in when I thought of the dream of us ending. Because I had no love for Peter at this point, it wasn't difficult to say goodbye to him over the phone. There was no fight left in me to try to reconcile with him. I should have been angry with him for lying to me about his business trip, but I was actually relieved to be out of the situation.

I held the secret of our breakup within me for a few days as I pondered what my next step would be. I feared criticism and backlash from my sister if I dared to tell her that Peter did not want me to return to the house. She already thought the whole notion of my moving to Florida to be with Peter was crazy. My intuition shouted that she would in no way be supportive. I needed a couple of days to myself to think through the situation. I had time on my side, since this was a long weekend visit. It was my prerogative to decide when, with whom, and how I chose to share this information, because I was already displaced and in a vulnerable situation. I chose to sit in silence and place a wall of protection around myself after Peter had wronged me on many levels.

After five days of a pleasant visit with my sister, which included a relaxing walk on the beach in Jupiter, she asked, "When do you think you're heading back to Peter's?"

"I don't have an answer at this moment," I replied. My intuition shouted, *Protect yourself; don't let her into this space yet*. However, my logical side thought, *The longer you put this off, the more difficult it will get*. I decided I couldn't put it off any longer.

I dreaded the next day. I mustered up the courage to ask my sister if I could stay with her for a few more weeks. I was in need of a temporary home. I had money in my account for an apartment rental. I needed to figure out where to live. I approached my sister as she worked in her home office. "I need to talk with you. Peter has made it quite clear that he doesn't want me to return to the house. He feels that it is best if I stay with you." Tears rolled down my cheeks.

I will never forget the look in her eyes. Without hesitating, she said coldly, "You cannot stay here. You have to go back to Peter's or get a motel room."

"Why? What have I done to you that you are not willing to help me?" I cried out in disbelief.

"You're such a risk-taker, coming to Florida. Now you have to pay the consequences for your decision to risk it all to be with Peter." She evaded my question about what I had done to offend her. She had no answer, because I had done nothing wrong to her. My intuition about how she would respond had been correct.

I felt the intense pain of abandonment that my own sister was throwing me onto the street. I had been a respectful sister in her home. We hadn't had any arguments or problems during my visit. I was heartbroken about the way my sister had responded.

Peter was just "a guy" I had known for a short time. He was the catalyst, the gateway to my new life in Florida. My sister, on the other hand, was someone I had loved my whole life, someone with whom I wholeheartedly believed I shared a deep bond. My sister's response showed no compassion. She didn't pause to think, *Let me give this some thought for a moment.* Nor did she respond, *I don't want you to ever have to go back to a raging alcoholic who screamed at you regularly.* No, she was definite about not letting me stay there. Devastated, I had nowhere to turn. I was new to Florida and needed guidance and help. Her boyfriend told me, "I'll drive you back to Peter's home."

"No, I'm not going back there," I replied. He followed my sister's lead in not offering me any help.

The cruel irony of the situation was that I had arranged for my sister to have a place to stay when she'd first arrived in Florida through my connection with my ex-boyfriend, Dominique. Dominique and I had lived together for five years in Philadelphia and Boston before he had moved to Florida. I had also paid for her one-way plane ticket to Florida. Additionally, years before she moved to Florida, I had provided her with a home to live with Dominique and me. She stayed with us in Boston for a year and a half, during which she paid no rent and no utilities. Yet I was denied any help during my crisis of need—not even a week or two of shelter.

In retrospect, I realize that a veil had been lifted. If Peter had not displaced me from the house, I would never have been exposed to this side of my sister. A truth had been revealed. She did not love me as I believed she did. No one who lived in a three-bedroom home with a guest bedroom could throw her sister onto the street for no justifiable reason. Yet when my mother, who owned her home in Pennsylvania, went through a terrible breakup with her live-in companion of seventeen years, my sister offered to let her live permanently with her and her boyfriend.

My sister denied me help because she had been led by fear. Fear drove her decision. She feared that I would become a financial burden on their lives. She forgot that I had spent most of my adult life as an independent woman. I learned that it is during our crises that we learn who is there for us and who isn't—in essence, who loves us. Even during one of the most painful abandonments in my life, **God revealed the promise of His presence in that He would never leave me nor abandon me**. "Be strong and of good courage, do not fear nor be afraid of them; for the Lord your God, He is the One who goes with you. He will not leave you nor forsake you" (Deuteronomy 31:6).

Crying hard, I was unable to think clearly at all. I prayed for God's help and guidance and then reached for my cell phone. I was led to call Dominique, my old friend and ex-boyfriend, who lived nearby in Palm Beach Gardens. I informed him that I had been displaced from both Peter's and my sister's homes. "Pack your stuff," Dominique said. "I'll be right there."

He picked me up, and I stashed my belongings in his car to go back with him to his condo. His car was filthy, and there were cigarette ashes all over the passenger seat. However dirty the interior of his car appeared, it didn't matter. Gratitude filled my heart for his friendship and help.

At first, Dominique's friendship comforted me. He lived with his mother on the first floor of a two-bedroom condo. He jokingly told the security gate guard upon our entrance to the condo, "I went to pick up my wife."

"Very funny, Dominique," I tried to say in a chipper voice to keep from breaking down. My heart ached, shocked and devastated by what had happened. I was indeed grateful that he cared enough to rescue me from my sister's home. Dominique had a kind heart in that he helped many people along their way, including my sister.

There was a long, awkward silence between us as we pulled up to his condo. "You know, Karen, I am appalled by your sister's behavior. I helped her twice in her life with a home both in Boston and Florida."

"Yes, isn't it ironic that you gave my sister a home for seven months during her transition to Florida and now you're helping me?" I replied.

I was unable to sleep that first night with Dominique in his queen-size bed. The black sheets we slept on appeared to not have been washed in months. There were food crumbs and cigarette ashes throughout the sheets. Although I was grateful to have a roof over my head, I had unknowingly walked into another nightmare.

After a sleepless night in his bedroom, I told Dominique, "I would be more comfortable sleeping on the sofa in the living room." It was a love seat, and it was too small for me to stretch my long legs out, but I needed to sleep alone. Even though Dominique had remained a gentleman and hadn't made any sexual advances, it still was an inappropriate sleeping situation.

The next afternoon, he asked what kind of groceries I wanted from the store. Before answering him, I eagerly shared my good news. "I have an interview lined up tomorrow for an assistant event planner position. However, as you know, my SUV is in Pennsylvania at my mother's. Could I borrow your car for the interview if you're not using it?"

"This event planner job you want is a scam," he said.

"No, it's not! I need to go check it out. I'm trying to put my life on track," I pleaded. "If you don't feel comfortable with me taking your car, please drive me. I'll give you gas money."

We got into an argument over the fact that I had tried to quickly land a job and he was preventing me from going to the interview. Trouble poured into the condo from our argument. He spoke to me in a condescending tone as if I were a naïve child. He eventually retreated into his bedroom. He never went to the grocery store either. Because no food was stocked in the house, all I found to eat for a few days were hot dogs in the fridge and oatmeal for breakfast. I had no transportation to the grocery store. I was in despair.

Luckily, Dominique's friend Peri knocked on the door. She introduced herself and we talked for a while. Peri lived upstairs in the condominium complex and had a sparkling southern personality. She invited me to her church, which was in a movie theater, for the Sunday service. I planned to go with her on Sunday morning. When we arrived at the church, I was introduced to other neighbors who lived a few doors down as well.

As the arguments escalated between Dominique and me, I questioned how everything had gone sour so quickly. Had I contributed to this downward spiral between Dominique and me? I knew I had been a respectful guest other than our not seeing eye to eye in regard to the interview. We also did not agree over the fact that Dominique tried to persuade me to take a plane back to my mother's home in Pennsylvania. He saw his idea as the only answer and the only way out of my dilemma. I refused to go along with his idea of flying back to Pennsylvania. I was determined to stay in Florida.

By now, my father was aware of the situation and quite concerned. He had asked me over the phone for Peter's phone number. My father called Peter and had a conversation with him in which he gave Peter "a piece of his mind." He clearly remembered Peter calling him and asking for his daughter's hand in marriage before my moving to Florida. It gave me quite a bit of comfort knowing that my dad was supportive and concerned about my situation. He also did not agree with the way my sister had handled the situation.

One evening, Charlotte, Dominique's kind mother, sat with me at the small, round kitchen table. She seemed troubled by the constant arguments in her home. Her kindness propelled me through many difficult days. I was thankful for her supportive presence. She shared with me in her charming French accent, "I don't know what is wrong with my son. He has always cared for you."

I didn't know how to respond to her, but it was evident that Dominique had changed from the years I had spent with him. He still had the same kind heart, but he had fallen into a downward spiral right before my eyes. Dominique had battled an alcohol addiction during the time I lived with him. After twenty-two years of knowing him, the consistent addiction took its toll on his mind and body. He seemed more anxious, irritable, and reclusive than when we lived together. I always felt compassion toward him because he suffered from bipolar disorder. Unfortunately, he never received the help he needed and self-medicated for relief. Sadly, he battled his own demons.

A realization came to me later. Dominique may have felt rejected by me without my even knowing it. Maybe that first night of the four days he helped me, he hoped we would be reconciled into a romantic relationship beyond just our friendship. I was too emotionally wounded from Peter and my sister to even consider a relationship deeper than a friendship with him.

The next day, the neighbors from a few doors down whom I had met in church invited me to a pasta dinner at their home. I was truthful with them about the strenuous situation with Dominique. They explained to me that I was in the midst of spiritual warfare, but that God would use this adversity to my advantage. After dinner, they prayed for me as we held hands in a circle. Their warmth and friendliness provided comfort and a break from the maze of darkness that surrounded me.

The next morning Peri left for work after overhearing Dominique argue with me through the kitchen window. Upon returning home from work, she invited me to stay for the night in her condo upstairs. I gladly accepted her compassionate invitation.

Earlier in the day, I called Kathy, an old high school friend, in Austin, Texas. I explained my dire situation to her. Kathy had lived in South Florida before moving to Texas. Through the grace of God, she had a connection in South Florida who could be of great help. Her friend Leah owned a few condos that were available on the beach in Lauderdale-by-the-Sea. This quaint town was forty-five minutes south of Palm Beach Gardens. I immediately called Leah, who, in return, e-mailed me pictures of the two vacant condos. The rest is history, as they say. Without seeing the condos in person, I informed her that I would be renting one of them. I had no choice. God, in His loving way, had opened a new door for me.

The following day, the neighbors from church who had prayed for me dropped me off at the train station. I will never forget the kindness of strangers. Additionally, I will never forget Peri's care and concern as she took me into her home for the night. I took the Tri Rail train from Palm Beach Gardens to Pompano Beach to meet with Leah, Kathy's friend. I was confident that one of the two condos would work out fine. With my suitcases packed, I was more than ready for my new home.

I will remember that day as long as I live. For you see, on my way to this new home, I saw a beautiful rainbow in the sky out of my train window. I was mesmerized by God's beauty as shown in this brilliant rainbow. I remembered wondering if anyone else on the train was witnessing what I was seeing in that moment. I saw this incredible rainbow as God's promise that He would never leave me nor abandon me. It was a sign from God that He was right there by my side.

God opened those doors so that within five days of my sister's betrayal, I was going to a new home on the beach. I can't even fathom how God had worked so swiftly on my behalf. That I have a Father God who loves me more than any human possibly could is at times hard to comprehend, but it is the truth. "Like the appearance of a rainbow in a cloud on a rainy day, so was the appearance of the brightness all around it. This was the appearance of the likeness of the glory of the Lord" (Ezekiel 1:28).

Despite the adversity and pain I had experienced during my early days assimilating into Florida, God was revealing a second promise through the storm. **God's promise to protect me as a shield** unveiled itself. "As for God, His way is perfect; the word of the Lord is proven; He is a shield to all who trust in Him. For who is God, except the Lord? And who is a rock, except our God? God is my strength and power, and He makes my way perfect" (2 Samuel 22:31–33).

God promises His presence always, through both my trials and my successes in life. God definitely made sure I was placed where I needed to be despite the painfully difficult circumstances I was in. I saw the light for the first time in more than a month of fear and darkness. Although I suffered abandonment, I never lost hope. I never turned to drugs or alcohol to cope. I clung to God's promises of His presence and His protection clearly stated in the Bible. I focused on His promise, not the problem.

As a result of God's promise of never abandoning me being fulfilled in my life, my trust in God naturally deepened. Although I did not understand why I had to endure this suffering, I trusted God to fight this battle for me. God uses our most difficult times to draw us near to Him. He desires that we be in close relationship with Him. This is why He sent His beloved son, Jesus, as a bridge to bring us into relationship with Him.

Although I couldn't see the final outcome during the darkness and pain, God had a better plan for me than I could have ever had on my own. Even though I endured betrayal and abandonment, I believed by faith that somehow God had my back. Victory triumphed over evil as God demonstrated His almighty power. He worked behind the scenes, connecting me with the right people. Inch by inch He led me to my destiny. God used the adversity of that painful experience to strengthen me, empower me, and prepare me for a new degree of fearless living.

# 4

## the Gift Arrives

I arrived with apprehension at the train station in Pompano Beach. I had never met Kathy's friend Leah, and I searched through the faces of the bystanders. Leah spotted me and greeted me with a warm smile. Relieved that she had followed through on her word of picking me up at the train station, I got in her car and we drove to the two condos on the beach. I took the smaller studio condo, knowing I could rent it for only a couple of months. Leah had made arrangements to rent it after my two-month stay. After all the heartache I had endured, I never would have imagined that my destiny included living in a home on the beach. God knew my needs in that nothing would make me happier than this home.

The beach has always been a special place of healing and joy to me. To have a view of the ocean from my dining room table was incredible. I called my friends with great joy and excitement about having moved to the beach. After two weeks of healing through relaxing on the beach and getting to know my neighbors, I decided it was time to find some work. I instantly found a job running the front desk as a hostess at a nearby upscale Japanese restaurant. Next, my mom, who had been my rock throughout this whole ordeal, sold my car in Pennsylvania to her friend Art and thus, mailed me a check. I bought a used car after searching a few local car dealerships. I no longer had to take the free shuttle bus for tourists back and forth for groceries and to work. Everything fell into place beautifully.

October 2010

Interestingly enough, once I was somewhat situated in my new temporary home, Peter's younger and only brother, Mike, called me. I told Mike that I was no longer living with Peter and told him about the horrible way in which it had ended. Mike reminded me of our prior conversation by saying, "I told you to call me if you had any trouble with my brother, Peter." I hadn't felt I could turn to Mike, since he was Peter's brother. I really didn't know him well enough and did not want to burden him with my problems. Hearing from Mike was a breath of fresh air and a comfort. I felt a strong connection to him and was attracted to him even though we hadn't met in person. We agreed to meet at a casual restaurant in Boca Raton.

I'll never forget the first time we met. We sat at a high-top table and shared stories, getting to know each other. We talked quite a bit about my journey from Peter's house to the beach. He was a great listener, and we spent hours sharing. It was an enjoyable first meeting—to the point that I actually lost track of time.

Our friendship grew quite naturally as I saw evidence from the beginning that he had a heart of gold. I wanted to know more about this man. I learned up front that Mike's values were the polar opposite of Peter's when it came to women. Peter needed dozens of women; Mike needed only one woman. As the sun's rays beamed across our table, Mike shared, "All you need is one good woman by your side."

I had fallen in love with a fairy-tale romance when Peter swept me off my feet, but Mike was the real deal. Solid, trustworthy, loyal, deep, and intelligent described Mike's character.

I had never met anyone like Mike. He had many special qualities that attracted me to him early on. I felt blessed that I had the honor and privilege of knowing him through a solid friendship. The qualities I admired most about him included his incredibly kind, generous acts of helping others in any way he could wherever he was placed.

I was excited every time Mike called me. I was not only attracted to his heart, but found myself physically attracted to him as well. He was handsome, with a perfect athletic build, salt-and-pepper hair, and expressive brown eyes. He had an inner and outer strength that was uniquely his. I loved that he not only made me feel safe with him, but that we had social chemistry in addition to physical chemistry. I simply loved how he made me feel happy when we were together. Although we were loyal to each other in the sense that we had no interest in dating other people, the lines between whether we were dating or enjoying a deep friendship were blurred occasionally. Neither he nor I was capable of jumping into a romantic relationship at the time, because we both needed time to heal from our recent past. Mike was grieving over the loss of his father. However, I hoped that our deep connection would blossom into a deeper loving relationship someday.

As Mike and I spent more time together and on the phone, I learned about his intriguing childhood through several endearing stories. One of my favorite stories was about when Mike, Peter, and their father were vacationing in a casino in Las Vegas. Mike was just a child, perhaps around ten years old. After his father dropped off Mike and Peter in the arcade room of the casino, he told them, "Anything you boys want for lunch, just charge it to the room." Well, Mike, with his generous heart, ordered hamburgers and milk shakes for all the kids in the arcade. He innocently wanted to share lunch with his new friends. After all, all he had to do was charge lunch to the hotel room. I can only imagine how his dad must have reacted when he received the bill at the time of checkout from the hotel. I'm sure his dad must have smiled, knowing his young son cared enough to provide lunch for all the kids.

The manner in which Mike grew up fascinated me. He and Peter, who was three and a half years older, were raised in a home with both a maid and a chauffeur. Life began for Michael on July 14, 1969, in Seoul, South Korea. His father, Pedro, was of Mexican descent, and his mother was of Irish descent. Tired of attending segregated schools in Texas, Pedro forged his mother's signature so he could join the army earlier than the legal age required. He met Mike's mother in Tokyo, where her father served in the air force. She worked as a hostess for a Japanese restaurant and had once appeared as a model in *Cosmopolitan* magazine in a feature on "an American in Japan."

Mike's father was an enlisted man in the army before his successful, adventurous career in the insurance business. Pedro sold life insurance policies to American soldiers in South Korea, and Michael lived his first three years there, until his parents divorced. He and Peter moved with their mother to the States, where she remarried. According to Peter, his mother remarried again and again, which paved the road to a painful childhood for both boys. Pedro considered having his mother raise the boys but ultimately decided that it was best for them to remain with their mother.

Michael's childhood was plagued with instability, as he not only moved frequently from home to home, but also had to adjust to new stepfathers. Mike had a hard time trusting people, which stemmed from his unstable childhood. His dad adored Mike as the favored son, and compensated for his distance overseas through generous financial provision.

All through high school at Stone Mountain High in Georgia, Michael had shown amazing talent as the star quarterback. In ninth grade, he advanced to the varsity football team as quarterback with his golden arm. He was truly a gifted athlete at an early age. I've never heard of any freshman in high school advancing to the varsity football team as the quarterback. Mike's advancement caused quite a stir, particularly with his jealous brother, Peter. Peter was also on the varsity football team but was not quite the athlete Mike was. Peter actually had his high school buddies rough up Mike by stuffing him into a large linen bag in the locker room one day after practice. Peter's envy of Mike's success caused him to bully his own brother.

This envy prompted Mike to quit the team until Peter graduated, because he did not want to outshine his brother. His football coach urged him to come back to the football team, but Mike waited. Mike's extraordinary heart showed love and loyalty to his brother despite his brother's envy. I believe that after all the hardship the brothers had endured in their childhood, Peter was all Mike had, since his father lived overseas. Deep down, Mike didn't want to alienate his brother.

Also during his freshman year, Mike was invited to three proms, evidence of how handsome and popular he was. Once Peter graduated from high school, Mike rejoined the football team. Even after daily practice was over, he would run up and down the hill repeatedly to strengthen his body before going home. He desired to be the best quarterback that he could be. Mike exuded confidence as the quarterback and leader of the team. He appeared to have a promising future, with his advanced athletic abilities.

Naturally, Michael received a football scholarship to college. He declined it in favor of remaining loyal to his high school sweetheart. His mother and stepfather, unsatisfied with Mike's response, kicked Mike out of the house for not accepting the college scholarship. He faced homelessness and lived out of his car with no job and no income just months out of high school. It was the dead of winter. He slept in the backseat of his car under a blanket. He showered at his girlfriend's home after her parents left for work every morning, and she cooked him breakfast daily. That was how Mike lived for several months.

Pedro, living in South Korea, had no idea about his son's struggles. He would have been on the first plane over to the States if he had known Mike was being treated that way. It must have been a painful experience for Mike, being rejected by his mom and stepdad. Mike was forced to survive on his own for the first time, with no direction. He struggled on the streets to survive. His pride kept him from calling his father. Perhaps he didn't know how to ask for help.

Meanwhile, Peter enjoyed college life in his fraternity at the University of Georgia. Mike eventually moved back to Seoul to be near his father, who helped him land a job as manager at Camp Casey of the USO. Mike enjoyed life in South Korea with his father close by and lived there for approximately ten years. Then Pedro's age and failing health dictated their return to the States. As his father's health deteriorated, Mike moved into his dad's condo in Boca Raton to care for him.

When I first became acquainted with Mike, I felt deep compassion toward him, as he was grieving his father's death in 2008, two years earlier. Mike and his dad were extremely close, and the loss of his father had come as a huge blow. His father had been his idol, whom he loved more than anyone on earth. Every year on Mike's birthday, Pedro would ask, "Where do you want to go for your birthday, Bing?" Bing was the beloved nickname his dad had given to Mike. Pedro owned a condo and two lots of land in Hawaii where they frequently traveled for a month's stay for Mike's birthday. Pedro had spoiled Mike, yet I sensed that he was humbled by his emotionally difficult childhood.

Mike was fluent in both English and Korean and spoke some Spanish and Japanese as well. His grandmother spoke only Spanish, so he learned the language at a young age. He had fond memories of his grandmother's love for cooking and how she made her meals from scratch. Perhaps Mike inherited his passion for cooking from her. He was a gifted chef and had worked in restaurants in the past.

Mike and I had similar parallels from our childhoods. He and Peter were three and a half years apart in age, just like my sister is three and a half years younger than me. We both were the products of difficult childhoods. My father and mother divorced when I was ten years old. My mother remarried once, and my father remarried twice. I, too, had to adapt to new stepmothers and a stepfather as well. Like Mike's father, my father was a successful businessman who spoiled my sister and me, particularly at Christmastime. My father used to send my sister and I back to the Philadelphia train station in the company limousine after holiday visits. I went to college at Penn State while my sister attended high school. We were raised by my mother and stepfather in a small steel town in central Pennsylvania where I very much enjoyed being a teenager. My father lived in an affluent area near the ocean, whereas my mother lived in a more rural area. Being exposed to both contrasting lifestyles made me into a better, well-rounded person.

Mike and Peter were complete opposites in every way. After years of working as a stockbroker, Peter paraded his objects of wealth, driving his Jaguar during the day and his Porsche at night, housing two cars in his garage. Mike saved his money. He didn't feel the need to purchase luxury items such as Rolex watches like his brother did. Peter was complicated; Mike was simple.

Of the two brothers, Mike was definitely more the "giver." It used to infuriate me that Peter called Mike only when he needed money or needed him to cook dinner to impress Peter's dates. Peter never called Mike out of concern to make sure he was okay. Mike, with his loyal, loving heart, rushed to Peter's side any-time his brother called.

Before I met Mike, he had been admitted to a local hospital for intense stomach pain. Mike claimed that his wallet, which contained a check from his inheri-tance made out to him for forty thousand dollars, had been stolen out of the drawer next to his bed in the hospital room. He had to stop payment on the check. Mike had been living off of the inheritance he received from his father. My second time of seeing him con-sisted of driving him back to the hospital, where he met with a police officer to report the theft of his wallet and check.

Although we barely knew each other, I had immedi-ately felt a sense of security and safety with him. Mike instinctively protected me wherever we went. Even when we crossed the street together, he would auto-matically extend his arm in front of me as oncoming cars approached us. I joked with him occasionally, "You know, I'm an adult who knows how to cross the street," even though deep down, I loved his natural protec-tive instinct. I had never had that type of protection before from a man. Particularly given all the hurt and betrayals I had endured recently, his protection comforted me more than he knew.

Mike had nowhere to stay until the incident of the stolen check was cleared up. I don't know where he was living at the time, but he had no car and no home, although he had large inheritance checks for living expenses. Because Mike needed a place to stay as his funds were tied up, I invited him to sleep on the sofa in my studio at the beach. He never once tried to hit on me. He was too much of a gentleman. We often stayed up late and discussed the Bible. I loved our late-night conversations about our faith. I barely even knew him, but I gave him a place to stay and lent him two hundred dollars. I e-mailed Peter and pleaded with him to take Mike into his home until Mike got his situation straightened out. Peter e-mailed me back that he did not wish to help Mike. I knew from the not-too-distant past how it felt to be in such a vulnerable homeless situation, and thus I empathized with Mike and opened my home for him to stay for as long as he needed to. After three or four nights, Mike left to take care of his personal business.

## November 2010

One evening, I was sitting outside by the pool of the rented studio, talking with Leah's husband, the owner of the condo, when I heard someone call, "Karen, Karen" from the other side of the fence. I looked over and couldn't believe it was Mike. He stood there in his brown leather jacket, looking relieved. Mike explained that he had walked twenty-three miles from Boca Raton to see me. I was stunned. Nobody had ever walked twenty-three miles to see me. He totally surprised me.

Gloria, my warm-hearted neighbor and coworker, invited us to go out for Thanksgiving. We went to a local sports bar/restaurant in Fort Lauderdale. She generously offered to pay for our dinners. Mike, whose funds were still tied up and who had no money, refused to eat. Gloria commented that he was too difficult. He definitely had a stubborn streak. Aside from being stubborn, Mike's pride dictated his choice not to eat because he was uncomfortable allowing a woman to pay for his Thanksgiving dinner. Perhaps it was the way his father had raised him. Mike was traditional in that he preferred to pay for dinner, particularly when in the presence of women.

One day when Mike and I were at the beach, I told him I wanted to build upper-body strength. We swam in the ocean together, and the salt water was warm. He grabbed my legs playfully and said, "Keep swimming with your upper body and arms. I've got your legs. We're going to build that upper-body strength you need."

After a while my arms naturally tired, and I shouted, "Okay, I'm done. I'm tired."

"Keep going," he replied. "You're doing great!" He knew exactly how to get me to where I needed to be. I adored that caring side of him.

### December 2010

Our evolving friendship grew beautifully for the first four months. The concept of being friends with a man first was new to me. I usually fall head over heels in love in relationships with men. When Mike and I first met, we were both coming from painful, vulnerable places. Mike's loss of his father and the betrayal I had experienced revealed that we needed time to heal and develop trust in our friendship first. All of the ingredients of love were there; we took our time in building a strong foundation.

My two-month agreement to rent the studio on the beach ended, and I needed a new place to live. I moved several miles out west to rent a room in a home in Tamarac. Mike called me every morning to see how I was. I felt his genuine care and concern for me, which touched me deeply. We met on my days off for a movie, dinner, or shopping at the mall. Mike always dressed impeccably. I loved his taste in clothes, particularly his button-down oxfords. I later learned that he had been voted "best dressed" by his senior high school classmates.

On Christmas Day we decided to go to the movies. With the background and passion I had for dance, I chose the movie *Black Swan*. Poor Mike had to endure a movie about the life of a ballerina, although it did have some dark twists to it. Toward the end of the movie, I wished that he would put his arm around me. He didn't. At that point, I had begun to develop deeper feelings for him and wanted a more romantic relationship.

### February 2011

The woman I rented from in Tamarac, Carolyn, explained to me that she was not legally allowed to

rent out a room because of the homeowner associa-
tion's rules. She told me about her dilemma a month
and a half after I'd moved into her home, although
she'd obviously known from the beginning that it was
illegal to rent to me. She was short of money, and in
addition to the rent, asked me to split the utility bills,
which she hadn't been clear about from the beginning. I refused to give in to her demands of splitting
the utility bills, and she threw a plastic measuring cup
across the kitchen floor in a temper tantrum. She also
threatened to change the locks on the front door. Her
behavior was a red flag to me that I needed the help
of the police. A police officer came to the house and
informed her of my rights as a tenant. Next, she called
her sister-in-law, Debbie, "the self-professed antichrist,"
to come and sleep over.

The next morning, Debbie tried to intimidate me
into leaving the house. She walked into my bathroom,
blowing cigarette smoke into my face. As I got ready
for work, she told me she was the antichrist. After the
betrayals and heartaches I had endured, her intimi-
dating antics had no effect on me. I was not intimi-
dated by her at all. It was uncomfortable, but I plowed
through the difficulty as I went about my business getting ready for work.

When I came home from work, Carolyn had
stripped the drapes off my bedroom window as well
as the comforter from my bed. Her goal was to make
me as uncomfortable as possible. Her juvenile antics
did not faze me. Having the promise of God's presence
with me at all times, I actually slept peacefully that
night. I chose to ignore her selfish, cruel acts, as my

past experiences had prepared me for fearless living. God uses our adversities to strengthen us. Before moving to Florida, this type of intimidation would have caused me great distress. However, I moved with grace and ease, thanks to God's presence and comfort.

Mike was concerned and protective about my circumstances in that house. He naturally came to my rescue. We had made the decision to live together. The crazy sister-in-law, Debbie, attempted to control the situation: she gave us a few leads from her computer in the house, and then followed Mike and me out the front door to my car as we left to look for apartments.

Her intention was to follow behind us in her car. She also tried to intimidate me again before I pulled out of the driveway when she said, "Don't try to lose me on the highway either." I thought to myself, *I would love nothing more than to lose you on the highway.* Nobody had invited her to come to look at apartments with us. It was actually none of her business, not to mention the fact that her behavior was psychotic. She followed us in her car and actually went with us to look at one apartment. We looked at a few more places after that, but nothing appealed to me.

Mike and I then packed my car with my belongings. We said pleasant goodbyes to them as if everything was all rosy. It wasn't. Carolyn and Debbie made my life a living hell with their immature, emotional reactions to the conflict. It appeared I was unable to leave the unending cycle of being without a home in South Florida. However, this time (unlike with my sister and Peter) I stood my ground. I did not let Carolyn push me around. I knew that although she had deceived me through an illegal rental, her cruel tactics would not make me leave the house before I was ready. I took a few days of prayer and talks with Mike before I came to any decisions. I began to pray every morning for not only guidance, but for wisdom and discernment.

I left a few days later, when I was ready, when the time was right for me. If I was being "tested," I knew I had learned a valuable lesson. God had shown me that not everyone was as nice as I had believed, but He equipped me with new strength. He showed me how to fight my battles through prayer first. I had learned not to be trusting of everyone. God had used my past adversity with Peter and my sister to grow me with new toughness. God made me like steel inside, unbreakable like a spiritual warrior.

Once again, although my future was unknown, I knew God's promise of protection quite well. God had placed Michael in my life. Mike was the gift. Ironically, our journey of living together began Valentine's Day weekend. Being the romantic that I am, Mike's love and loyalty was the best Valentine's Day gift I could have had.

With my car packed with all my belongings, we drove off into the gorgeous sunset with no idea whatsoever where we would be living. I felt so alive. We decided to stop at the casino in Coconut Creek. Neither one of us was into gambling, but we had a fun evening, a great time. We then stayed in a hotel for the night. The next night we moved to another hotel and stayed for several nights. I grew to love living in hotels. Life was full of spontaneous adventures with Mike by my side.

# 5

## *Let Your Light Shine*

❦

**March 2011**

M ike and I eventually settled in Deerfield Beach, where we stayed in a long-term hotel with a monthly rate. After we had settled in, we learned that drug dealers and prostitutes occasionally roamed around there at night. I had never lived anywhere where dark characters resided. I found myself curious to see and experience how people like that lived, yet I was not attracted to a dark path by any means. It was as if I had a piercing view of these characters through the lens of a camera. Perhaps I was intrigued by danger on some level, although I was never afraid during the four months I lived there. I had never felt as safe and protected by a man in all my life as I did with Mike.

College kids on spring break also stayed in the hotel. The hotel atmosphere was a terrible influence on Mike. I had seen him remain sober during the blossoming of our relationship before we lived together. Unfortunately, he fell back into his old ways of drinking alcohol and occasionally smoking cigarettes. I never really drank or did drugs of any kind while with Mike. I just drank socially occasionally when we went out to dinner.

Several men and women in the hotel ran around daily looking for Roxys, "the blue synthetic heroin pill." I had never heard of Roxy until I moved there. It saddened me to see so many lives plagued by addictions. Mike once boasted to our neighbor, "I am proud that the woman I am with has no addiction to any of that garbage."

It was, at times, like a dorm room where neighbors occasionally stopped by for cigarettes and so on. Mostly they befriended us because they knew Mike had money. He had received an inheritance after his father passed away. They were all financially struggling to make ends meet. Mike, with his giving heart, genuinely wanted to help others. Living there showed me the kind of generous, pure heart Mike had.

One day, he helped a young stranger about to be evicted with two hundred dollars. He never received the money back. Mike used money to bless people. I also witnessed Mike's generosity with a tip he left for a server in a diner. Mike paid for my hot turkey sandwich, which came to about seven dollars and some change. After we walked out of the restaurant, the female server ran out and shouted, "Sir, you left your change."

Mike replied, "No, that's for you, sweetheart." He had left a twenty-dollar bill to cover a seven-dollar sandwich.

I asked him, "Why did you leave such a generous tip? Did you think her service was that great?"

He answered, "Karen, you never know. Perhaps that server could be financially struggling to take care of three kids on her own." Mike didn't care about money. He used it to help others.

I will never forget as long as I live Mike's incredibly kind act of helping a stranger in need. One of our neighbors, who was broke with no car, had to go to the emergency room. Mike offered to drive him to the hospital in my car. What really astounded me was that he not only drove him to the emergency room, but stayed in the waiting room for three hours to be supportive to this stranger. I would give any person a ride to the emergency room, but I honestly don't know that I would wait for three hours with a total stranger in the waiting room. That was Mike, though. He put other people first, before himself. After witnessing many needs of our neighbors, I believe that God placed us in that strange hotel of darkness to be a light and help to others.

Spring was in the air, and there was a feeling of newness and warmth as the sun radiated more strongly. Yes, it may be hard to believe, but even Florida goes through changes in seasons. Easter morning, Mike brought me some Easter lilies that I truly wanted. He also thoughtfully bought lilies for the maid who serviced our room. Early that afternoon, Mike and I dined in an upscale seafood restaurant on the Intracoastal Waterway for our Easter dinner. I wore a beautiful floral dress, and Mike dressed nicely as well. We had a fantastic water-view table as boats glided on the waterway. A neighbor in the hotel worked there as a chef.

We were madly in love during the springtime. We truly loved each other. Before we fell asleep every night, we lay in each other's arms. I placed my hand over his heart. He would then rest his hand on top of my hand as we drifted to sleep.

We frequently visited the nearby beach early in the evenings. Mike and I strolled along the path as we watched the soft colors of the sunset melt behind the palm trees. I loved it when he held my hand. I felt his love and strength in his healing hands. I felt at one with him like I had never felt with anyone before. Once he stopped and said to me, "If all it takes to make you happy is going to the beach, then I'm the luckiest guy in the world." Joy and happiness radiated from me during those days. I felt incredibly alive at this time in my life. It didn't matter that our hotel room wasn't the most luxurious. I was with Mike, and that was all that mattered.

In his usual protective mode, Mike waited outside the hotel door every night when I came home from work. He took up a friend, José, and they occasionally went out at night to play pool and have a few drinks. Of course, as much as we were in love, like all couples, we had our occasional arguments. One night, Mike didn't come home because of an earlier argument. José tried to comfort me as tears rolled down my cheeks. Initially, I didn't know what had happened to Mike. I learned the next morning from José that Mike had checked into a hotel down the street for the night. José offered to get Mike and bring him home. In the pit of my stomach, I knew I shouldn't trust José with the keys to my car, but I was desperate for Mike to come home to our humble hotel room.

Of course, José got into a minor car accident while driving my car. Unbeknownst to me, his driver's license had been suspended. When I arrived at the scene of the accident, José was in the backseat of the police car in handcuffs. I was mad at Mike for all the chaos, although in retrospect, I took responsibility for the mistake I'd made in giving José the keys to my car. I should have driven José to the hotel where Mike was staying. Lesson learned, period.

Mike enjoyed his new friendship with José. He knew José struggled to take care of his wife and their two-year-old. Mike once took José's wife to a store and bought her food for her toddler. He also bought their daughter a floating device for the hotel pool. I loved how Mike's light shined as he helped our neighbors. With my natural love for children, I offered to babysit their daughter so they could have a night out together.

José once commented, "The two of you are like an old-fashioned, traditional couple. You two really care in that you both actually listen and look people straight in the eye when talking." God sent Mike to be a light to our neighbors in the hotel. I learned who Mike's essence truly was during those days. He inspired me to become more generous with helping others with my time and money. Mike's heart purely loved others. He consistently cared about providing help to his fellow neighbors on a day-to-day basis however he could.

# 6

*Jailhouse Blues*

Happily in love, I came home one night exhausted from work. Mike never came home that evening. Excessive worry ran rampant through my mind. I tried to reach him on his cell phone incessantly, but kept getting his voice mail. There were no clues about his disappearance. I knew he wasn't the type of man who chased women at all hours of the night. I barely slept a wink as angst hovered in the air.

I woke up the next morning with knots in the pit of my stomach. I was a nervous wreck as I realized that Mike had vanished without a trace. I called one of his friends, who advised me to check with the local hospitals as well as the local jail.

Sure enough, Mike had spent the night in jail. He had been arrested for possession of his antidepressant pills (which were not in the prescription bottle) and oxycodone. During the time I lived with Mike, he never abused drugs. His drug of choice was alcohol. He claimed that his friend José had had no pockets in the shorts he was wearing. Mike had offered to hold José's loose pills in addition to Mike's own antidepressants.

The antidepressants were legitimate: Mike suffered from depression after his father's death and was under the care of a doctor who had given him a prescription for them. In the state of Florida, it is illegal to carry loose prescription pills in one's pocket. They are required to be in the prescription bottle at all times.

Mike was arrested after engaging in a verbal confrontation with the clerk at the drugstore across from our hotel. Although it wasn't a physical fight, it was clear that Mike and José's drinking had led to trouble. Mike became argumentative from the alcohol. His mouth, not the loose pills, proved to be his downfall in that particular situation.

The profound wisdom from the book of Proverbs clearly says that the mouth can bless or curse. "Death and life are in the power of the tongue" (Proverbs 18:21). The Bible says that our words are always leading us somewhere. Mike's angry words led him to jail.

The next evening after work, I drove at midnight to meet with a female bond agent at her office. I was greeted by Jacquelyn, a woman with short blond hair and a no-nonsense personality. I showed her proof of collateral in exchange for a six-thousand-dollar bond for Mike's release from jail. Mike was released on bail as he awaited his trial.

We met with Jacquelyn after Mike's release the next day. He handed her a cashier's check for six thousand dollars. She gave us the name of a person who she said was a good local attorney to represent Mike's case. We chose an attorney based on her recommendation, which turned out to be a horrible mistake. The attorney basically took Mike's money up front and accomplished very little for him. Mike would have been better off with a public defender.

I faxed the antidepressant prescription from his psychiatrist to the attorney. To this day, I have no idea if the attorney actually sent the prescription information over to the court. The attorney claimed that he did. Mike was sentenced to participate in drug court, a substance abuse program, since this was his first offense with a drug charge. He was mad that the charges were not dropped. Mike was never charged with "intent to sell" drugs because it was only a few loose pills in his pocket. His attorney urged him to complete the program regardless of whether the verdict from the judge was fair or unfair.

Michael was stubborn at times. He tried to escape the pressure of the drug court system by drinking heavily. Once the court system got a grip on him for this nonviolent, low-level drug offense, there was no escape. South Florida already had an overload of systemic drug offenders. By 2016, Broward County, Florida (the county in which we lived) had the highest incidence of prescription drug abuse in the nation. However, criminalizing addicts is not working either.

**May 2011**

I knew the sentencing Michael had received was unfair. Life is unfair. I knew that God was in control of the situation. I believed with all my heart that God would see us through this heartache. I also believed that God used corrective measures just as any loving father would to help Mike grow and learn. Mike became angry and argumentative when he drank, and I hoped he would learn from this mess by living more wisely. We all make mistakes. I surely have made mistakes in my life as well. Although Michael wholeheartedly believed in Christ and the word of God, he lived rebelliously with his out-of-control drinking.

A neighbor from the hotel knocked on our door one morning. He shared a story from the local newspaper about a hotel on the Intracoastal Waterway in Pompano Beach that was not only beautiful, but offered monthly rates. Excited, we packed our belongings and left as soon as possible. I eagerly awaited our new home, because the people at our current hotel were a terrible influence on Mike. Later I learned that the hotel from hell had been shut down and condemned. I wondered what had happened to the many desperate people who were long-term residents there.

Mike and I enjoyed our new life in an upscale, higher-end hotel on the Intracoastal Waterway in Pompano Beach. After our prior living situation, this place seemed like paradise. From our room, we had a beautiful view of the Intracoastal and the pool. I grew to love the hotel life. Daily maid service, an exciting feeling of being on vacation, and eating most of our meals in restaurants thrilled me. I have to admit that I grew accustomed to this unusual, lavish lifestyle. It excited me. I always found living in the suburbs to be boring, although interestingly enough, that was how I had been raised.

Once we settled into our new hotel, Mike received a phone call from his brother, Peter. Peter asked Mike to lend him five hundred dollars. Mike asked me to lend him the money for his brother. Surely Mike had not forgotten how Peter had ousted me from his home ten months earlier. Mike knew how Peter and I had ended. Now I was to help Peter behind the scenes, lending him money? Why had Mike asked me to lend him money for his brother? I questioned his request, knowing that Mike had received an inheritance from his father's many properties—an inheritance that was paying for our current resort lifestyle. I felt Mike was testing me to see if I trusted him and decided to lend him the money for Peter.

When Mike and I drove to Peter's home, Peter did not know that Mike and I lived together. Mike hadn't yet told him that we loved each other. Mike said firmly, "Karen, wait here in the car. I'll be right out."

"Really, Mike? It's time to tell Peter the truth about us," I replied emphatically.

"Now is not the time," Mike said as he left the car.

I agreed and waited in the car in front of Peter's house while Mike ran in to lend his brother the money. The thought had occurred to me, *I could go ring the doorbell and let Peter know that I'm with Mike and that the money is coming from me.* However, my better judgment told me to wait until Mike felt it was the right time for Peter to know about us.

Mike entered his brother's home. While he was there, Peter gave Mike their dad's ring to keep. Additionally, he gave Mike his own Ferrari watch as collateral until he could repay the loan. Mike placed the watch in a safety deposit box in his bank, to be stored there until Peter paid him back. Mike never took off his father's white jade ring once he placed it on his right index finger. He loved the ring because it reminded him of his beloved father. I don't believe Peter ever did come to know that I was the one who initially lent him the money.

Even though I sensed that Peter took advantage of Mike at times, it seemed both brothers were comfortable with their roles. Peter was all the family Mike had other than his cousin Melanie. Mike's loyalty showed that he did whatever it took to keep his brother close.

My decision to trust Mike proved correct: he paid me back within the week along with interest to make it worth my while. Additionally, to my surprise, Mike opened up a checking account in my name. He deposited slightly more than twenty thousand dollars into the account. Our trust inevitably deepened. He entrusted me to take care of the household expenses and bills.

Meanwhile, Mike dealt with his weekly drug court program from his sentence. He was scheduled to attend drug court counseling and classes a couple of times a week. He attended occasionally but never consistently, which was in violation of his sentence. He also consumed beer before going to his classes.

Before I dropped him off in the parking lot for class one afternoon, he pulled out his mouthwash to cover up the smell of alcohol. Drug court had mandatory drug testing, and Mike came up clean. However, he would have failed miserably if they had tested him for alcohol. Although he was under court order to attend, he eventually stopped going altogether. Drug court was the sentence he had received in lieu of jail time. The jails were overcrowded, and this was a standard alternative program. Although Mike's addiction was to alcohol, I had hoped this program would help him.

Additionally, Mike missed his court date, which was intended to monitor his progress in the drug abuse program. His absence from court generated a warrant for his arrest. His beer consumption intensified because of the new pressure he faced with the warrant. He had reached a new level of addiction by consuming twenty-four to twenty-eight beers a day. Clearly, Mike was running from his problems instead of facing them directly.

Not only did Mike's drinking increase because of the pressure of having missed court, but our arguments escalated as well. He displayed ridiculous anger during our arguments. The worst argument, at the time, stemmed from Mike demanding that I close the account that he had opened for us under my name and return the money to him. I thought that given his drunken condition, he was incapable of handling money.

This was where living together got murky. The lines around the roles we played got blurry. Of course we loved each other and considered ourselves a married couple (although we were not legally married). Not only did we see ourselves as married, but so did our friends. A store clerk once said, "Your husband is waiting for you over by the door." Of course, others out in the world could sense our unbreakable bond as well.

I tried to justify our living together with the notion that we loved each other and were loyal to each other. However, through this experience, I learned and now understand why God wants us to live in marriage and not "just live together." God loves His children and wants the best for us. God knows that the pitfalls of "living together" cause unnecessary insecurities and confusion that marriage resolves.

Deep down, I felt the need to be in control as my environment with Mike spiraled out of control. Money was a tool I used to control the situation. Although he demanded that I return the money, I contributed to the argument by refusing to do so, because of his drunken state, which caused him to get even angrier. He threatened to throw my clothes into the hallway of the hotel and my laptop computer off the balcony during those crazy arguments. Of course, he was only releasing hot air. He never went through with any of his ridiculous threats.

The bottom line entered into the equation that I had had enough of the threats. I called hotel security and had him thrown out of the hotel. He was not allowed to return. He called and pleaded with me, saying he would get sober and straighten up. Even though I had every right to be mad at him for his horrible behavior, I never stayed mad at him for long. I had a soft spot in my heart for him. I also knew that I, too, was wrong for not returning the money. Additionally, I knew deep down that this was just bad behavior. Mike, at his essence when he was sober, proved to be a loving, kind man. That is what drove me to stay with him. I knew the sober man I had fallen in love with had seeds of greatness in him.

After he was banned from the hotel, I missed his presence. After all, I loved him deeply. I thought to myself, *I can't stand the idea of being away from Mike for even a night.* A week later, I decided to sneak him back into our hotel room. Of course, we couldn't enter through the front lobby area. After the security guard finished patrolling the grounds near the hotel pool around midnight, I quietly took Mike through the pool area and used the back doors to sneak him into the room.

We couldn't continue living there long term, because he was banned from the hotel. We found a smaller motel across from the beach a few blocks away.

I never understood how the alcoholism affected Mike's thinking process during those crazy arguments. However, his alcoholism affected his brain chemistry, which affected his judgment.

Once we were settled into our new place, I asked Mike, "Why did you make those juvenile threats to me? You never behaved like that before."

"I'm sorry," Mike replied. "I acted impulsively. I don't know what took over me. I'm under a lot of stress in that I missed court." His tone was sincere.

I didn't fully grasp it at the time, but I now believe Mike had attention deficit disorder. From watching a PBS educational program on ADD, I realized that I, too, possess traits of an adult with a mild case of ADD. Sadly, those with ADD need constant stimulation. They will find it any way they can, even through ridiculous arguments and debates.

Even though Mike's behavior was unlovable in those moments, I gave him another chance. I knew that God forgave me for all of my mistakes. I, too, was to forgive. In addition to forgiving Mike, I felt God in my spirit wanted me to forgive my sister for her betrayal. I asked God to show me how to forgive, because I needed help in this area. It took quite a bit of time to forgive my sister. It was no easy task. Although I no longer carried resentment toward her, because I forgave her, I would also never forget what she had done. God commands us to forgive those who have wronged us, although God does not want us to live in abusive situations. **God's promise of forgiveness** was etched into my heart. "Condemn not, and you shall not be condemned. Forgive, and you will be forgiven" (Luke 6:37).

Just a few days after we moved, my mother and sister came for a visit to take me to lunch. I had told my family that I no longer lived with Mike and that I lived alone in the motel. I felt Mike was too drunk for them to be around. He became belligerent at times in his heavy state of drunkenness. I felt I could handle him, but I needed to protect my family from him.

Mike left for a walk before my family arrived. I felt terrible about my decision to exclude him from lunch. However, given the circumstances with his heavy drinking, I felt it was best for everyone if he didn't join us. Mike didn't appear to care one way or the other about lunch with my family.

On a Sunday afternoon, we had lunch at the large Japanese restaurant where I worked. After we overstuffed ourselves, we drove back to the motel and took family photos in the beautiful garden in the back of that charming place. Despite the past arguments with Mike, I glowed with happiness in the photos. I loved living with Mike on the beach. I loved that my sister and I were reunited. I was grateful indeed for God's blessings upon my life.

I was also grateful for my job running the front of the restaurant. Being college educated, I never thought when I started the job that I'd work at the restaurant for more than three months. However, God had a plan for me after initially being displaced from Peter's home.

When I worked as a self-employed dance educator for twelve years in Rhode Island before moving to Florida in 2010, I felt that restaurant work was beneath me. I know it displeases God when we carry too much pride. I didn't know at the time I carried pride. God placed the gift of service in me: I love helping people. At the restaurant, my gifts were matched with the job. I strived to help people create great experiences and memories.

I also learned during that time that I thrived in an environment with people from various backgrounds. Working there energized me, because I enjoyed problem solving. I also loved the front-of-the-house staff and the managers. Not only did I enjoy the social aspect of it, but I earned a living while having fun every day. It definitely took me back to my younger, carefree days, and I wanted to bottle that feeling. In summary, God liberated me through the job by not only humbling me, but showing me that there was much more to life than falsely identifying through any position or title of being self-employed. God loves to grow us where we need it.

After we took photos in the garden of the motel, we went inside and sat on the wicker chairs across from the twin beds in the motel room. My sister noticed a couple of beer bottles on the nightstand next to one of the beds. "Those bottles were not there before we left," she said.

I quickly dismissed her comment. "Perhaps the maid found the bottles under the bed while we were out to lunch and forgot to throw them out." I was not up front with my sister even though I knew they were Mike's beer bottles. Mike had returned to the motel room while we were out to lunch. I thought to myself, *Oh, what a tangled web we weave, when first we practice to deceive.* I felt ashamed that I wasn't more honest with them. I had decided to keep my private life with Mike a secret from my family. I tried to shield and protect them from Mike's anger. My perfectionism ruled as I tried to create the appearance that all was well within my world. My family never did meet Mike that afternoon. They had no clue how deeply in love I was with a man whose alcohol addiction was spiraling completely out of control.

# 7

## *Miracle on Sixth Avenue*

❦

**August 2011**

Although I loved Mike with all of my being, I decided it was best to separate from him and his drinking. Mike's anxiety over having missed his court date drove him to drink excessive amounts of alcohol that weren't healthy for him or for me. I decided to live alone. I had a heart-to-heart conversation with Mike and told him I needed space apart from him. I gave Mike the money back, handing him a twenty-thousand-dollar cashier's check. I won't deny that I wanted to keep the money as a security blanket. However, it was the right thing to do, because initially it had been his money.

I found a studio apartment right in the area two blocks from the beach and near where I worked. The large apartment building had a beautifully landscaped exterior that caught my eye immediately. There were beautiful water fountains with stone paths under unique, old trees.

As hard as it was to be away from Mike, I tried my best to move on without him. He moved into an inexpensive motel down the street. In some strange way, it comforted me knowing that he was near me, even though I refused to live with him, given his condition.

One day after I had made the decision to live alone, I was driving home after an errand when I found Mike exhausted and intoxicated, sitting on a street corner. I drove him back to his motel and dropped him off. I helped him onto the bed, knowing he was ready to pass out at any moment. I took off his white sneakers and laid them near his suitcase. As I headed for the door to leave, his loving brown eyes penetrated me and he said, "You know we belong together." His words pierced my heart. His eyes then rolled back and closed as he passed out. I left for my new home, one block over from where he was staying.

The truth is I could never stay away from Mike for very long. I loved him with all my heart. I softened my position because I missed him terribly. Before long, we were together again. Mike moved into my studio, which had a separate kitchen, unlike our past hotel rooms, which hadn't had kitchens. Mike returned to his love of cooking as we created our little nest together. He was an amazing cook. Cooking was never my forte, but Mike was gifted with his passion.

At times when Mike and I slept together, it was as if I were sleeping next to a furnace. I never knew anybody's body temperature could be that hot without them having a fever. I assumed it was from the alcohol being processed in his body at night.

With Mike's warm heart, he made friends easily no matter where we moved. Our next door neighbor, Giovanni, and Mike spent time by the pool. They mixed cocktails and discussed life's matters. One night, Giovanni told me privately, "Mike loves you very much. His eyes water every time he talks about you." I knew Mike's emotions ran deeply, but I didn't know he expressed himself that way with his friends. Not only had Mike felt life deeply, but he reached out to others' needs as he felt their pain. He consistently showed himself to be a compassionate giver everywhere we went.

One night after I returned home from work, my legs were tired. We lived across the street from the drugstore. I asked Mike, "Would you give me a piggyback ride to the drugstore? My legs hurt." He carried me all the way to the drugstore. Giovanni laughed as he watched Mike carry me and the way we lovingly interacted with each other.

Life with an alcoholic was like a roller-coaster ride. We certainly had our share of ups and downs, but our love for each other created an unbreakable bond. I never knew what to expect from day to day with Mike. Even though he had an unpredictable side, I felt protected and safe with him. He brought out the free-spirited side of me.

I remained loyal to him even though he gave me a hard time too often while under the influence of alcohol. Once he ranted and raved after I had come out of a convenience store with the wrong kind of mushroom soup for him. I told him, "You buy your own soup next time!"

One afternoon after we had a horrible argument, Mike asked me to drive him to a dive motel several miles west of the beach. He was practically the only nontrucker at this seedy place. He felt he needed to get away and have some time alone. The pendulum swung once again, but this time, he left me. I hated the notion of being away from him, but deep down I knew his alcoholism was wreaking havoc on our lives. After I dropped him off, I was concerned about his safety because of the area around the motel. This one wasn't like the tourist-type beach hotels we had lived in.

The next morning, I called Mike on his cell phone. When I couldn't reach him, I called the front desk of the motel. The front desk clerk informed me that Mike had been arrested. How had he gotten arrested in only one night away? I later learned that this particular motel does background checks on all its guests. Sure enough, the warrant out for his arrest for missing his court date had finally caught up with him. God knew I had tried to warn Mike to give himself up, but Mike never listened to reason. His default in difficult times was to run, because at heart, he leaned on his own abilities in life. Even though Mike knew and believed in God, he relied more on himself than he did on God to see him through his difficulties.

## April 2012

The first time I visited Mike in jail was painful. I waited in a lobby for what seemed like forever. The personnel treated me like I was nothing more than a number. It broke my heart to see him incarcerated. I hated being away from him. I felt this emptiness inside of me, as if my other half weren't there. I also felt a sense of injustice that Mike was incarcerated, even though he had chosen his path. Yes, his alcoholism exacerbated the verbal argument with the drugstore clerk that had led to his arrest for having a couple of loose pills in his pocket. Yes, the situation escalated because he refused to deal with the sentencing that required him to attend drug court. Missing his court date ultimately led to the warrant, which led to his arrest. The only value I found in him being incarcerated was that it kept him sober.

I moved out of the efficiency in Pompano Beach to a new home in Fort Lauderdale with Diane. Diane became a friend after I rented from her in the home that we shared. She also rented another bedroom to her friend Ellen. We all spent time together socializing by going to brunch, dinners, and shopping. I also took Ellen to the beach. That was how I passed my free time when I wasn't visiting Mike in jail.

Mike served about four months in jail. He had lost his six-thousand-dollar bond to the bondsman because of a couple of missed court dates. All of those irresponsible, reckless decisions infuriated me at times.

After his initial arrest and bonding out of jail, Mike offered me half of the bond money, which was three thousand dollars. He had repeated his generous offer of gratitude for my help in getting him released at least a half dozen times. When he was incarcerated later, I needed money to move. I also needed money for minor medical bills. I withdrew the money first before talking to him about it. I thought Mike would understand my decision and that it would be best to explain everything once he was out of jail. His arrest had placed me in a difficult situation. I made a bad decision at the time that I would later regret.

After Mike was released from jail, he was extremely angry with me for not telling him about the money I had withdrawn. The truth was that if I had only been up front with Mike while he was in jail, he would have told me to take out the money I needed. He always gave me everything I asked for. In the past when we lived together, he had once said, "Do I ever deny you anything?"

This was a hard lesson that I had to learn. After everything we had been through, I broke a trust with him. Both Mike and I were at fault. He made many false promises under the influence of alcohol. I didn't know at the time that this is a common trait among alcoholics. He had also given a real estate agent a deposit on an oceanfront condo we were to rent. With my perfect credit score, Mike had me sign a lease for six months. He had offered to pay the six months' rent up front so that I would be comfortable. He put a nine-hundred-dollar deposit on the condo. Because I had and still have a stellar credit score, I could rent anywhere I wanted.

Mike even joked with the real estate agent during our meeting, saying, "Karen has the perfect credit score, and I'm the one with the money." However, because of Mike's arrest, I was unable to afford and thus move into the beachfront condo without him.

The condo owner threatened to sue me since I had already signed the paperwork for the lease. The owner expected me to pay all six months of rent up front as Mike had offered under the influence. Luckily, under God's protection, there never was a lawsuit against me. Although Mike initially lost the deposit, I retrieved it several months later.

However, I wasn't out of the woods yet. Mike was released in July 2012 after completing a monthlong substance abuse program for addiction. Participation in the program was part of his jail sentence, which satisfied the court. After his release, Mike learned that I had withdrawn the money he had offered me from his account. He remained mad at me to the point that he didn't call me to discuss it, as I had assumed he would. Actually, he never called me at all after he was released from jail.

I felt tremendous guilt along with the anguish and suffering I had endured with what transpired. I couldn't reach Mike by phone because he had changed his number. He no longer wanted contact with me. I called Colleen, Peter's girlfriend, who lived with him at the time. Colleen said, "I'm sorry, Karen. Mike doesn't want you to have his phone number."

To say I became upset and depressed would be an understatement. My sleep became erratic, and I frequently slept until noon. I didn't like being without Mike. I suffered during that time away from him. I prayed to God fervently, asking Him to forgive me for my foolish decision that had created turmoil. I had learned during that period that I had not trusted God for His provision. I repented and promised God that I would never take money like that again. God, in His gracious ways, forgave me and pressed upon me to ask Mike for his forgiveness.

However, how could I ask Mike for his forgiveness when I had no idea how to reach him?

Waiting. Waiting. Waiting. "Lord, how long must I wait? Please bring Mike back into my life," I cried out in prayer. I missed the sound of Mike's voice, his touch, and his strength. When Mike placed his arm around me, it was a feeling that I loved to feel. Words could never articulate that feeling of joy. What seemed like an eternity of waiting was really a lesson in patience and God's timing. I turned to read several uplifting psalms in scripture for relief of my pain.

One Sunday, I was alone in the house where I rented from Diane in Fort Lauderdale. I danced freely to a psalm from the Bible on the wooden floor in the living room. The floor and the large, antique mirror reminded me of an old dance studio from when I lived in Boston. As I choreographed dance moves to the psalm, I praised God through worship in a new way. I had never danced to a psalm before. It was a totally spontaneous and authentic moment.

Later that afternoon, I went to a store in a plaza near where I lived to return a shirt. As I started to shut the car off, an old R&B song came on the radio that caught my attention. I sat in the car a few extra minutes, listening to the song, and lo and behold, Mike appeared from around the corner. Mike walked right in front of my car. I couldn't believe my eyes as I witnessed a miracle from God.

God knew that I desperately desired to reach Michael somehow, since all of my efforts had been thwarted. With the hundreds of shopping plazas in South Florida, a densely populated area, the fact that Mike and I crossed paths astounded me. No doubt God had intervened so that destiny could play its hand. Mike stopped after he recognized me. I must have had the smile of the century and joy written all over my face when I stepped out of the car to approach him.

However, he didn't show the same joy as I did. He was pleasant in his humble demeanor, but I read in his face that he was still disappointed in me about the money, and rightfully so. I felt intensely happy to see him. Even though it was for only a few minutes, it made my day. I totally lit up like a Christmas tree.

After being released from the substance abuse program, Mike had remained sober and on a new path. That day, he was leaving the gym, which happened to be next to the women's clothing store where I needed to make the return. What if I had left my house fifteen minutes later? What if I had not listened to the song in the car and gone straight into the women's clothing store? I would not have seen Mike. One has to understand that the precise timing of our crossing paths was down to the seconds. I knew that we were meant to be. I had to be patient and give the relationship time.

A few weeks later, we crossed paths a second time near the same plaza. It was nighttime as I left the drugstore after running an errand. I saw a man with a red shirt walking in the rain. As I pulled out of the parking lot to turn onto the street, I saw that it was Mike. Rain pounded the pavement. I quickly rolled down the window on the passenger side and shouted, "Mike, get in. I'll take you wherever you need to go."

Mike said, "You can drop me off at the church on the corner."

I replied in amazement, "Mike, you live in this neighborhood too? I live diagonally two streets over from the church with Diane. I can't believe you rented a place in my neighborhood after you were released from the substance abuse program in jail." I continued, "You didn't know where I lived, and I couldn't find you either. You changed your phone number, and I had no idea where you were."

Again, not to be repetitive, but with all of the towns and cities in South Florida, Mike happened to rent a home only a couple of blocks from mine? Actually, it was no coincidence that God placed us so close together. I witnessed a second miracle.

**The promise from God's Word of waiting upon the Lord** was fulfilled in my life. "Therefore the Lord will wait, that He may be gracious to you; And therefore He will be exalted, that He may have mercy on you. For the Lord is a God of justice; blessed are all those who wait for Him" (Isaiah 30:18). It was mind boggling that we were neighbors without even knowing it until the second time we crossed paths. As hard as those long days of waiting for an answer about when I would see Mike again were, God's timing was perfect. God was absolutely in control.

# 8

## Reunited, and It Feels So Good

**October 2012**

On a laid-back Sunday afternoon, I relaxed on the beach, listening to the sounds of the gentle surf. My cell phone rang. Mike called me from his hotel room. He sounded terrible. "Peter and I had an argument," he said. "Not only did Peter tell me to leave the house, but he had my name removed from the permanent list of visitors at the security gate. I don't even care if I live anymore." He sounded suicidal. I had never heard Mike talk that way before.

"Mike, I'll be right there. What hotel are you in and what is the room number?" I asked with a sense of urgency. I quickly gathered my beach towel and straw tote bag and left the beach. I jumped into my car and drove quickly.

Mike had finally told Peter that we loved each other. Peter had just recently learned that we were a couple, although that was not the main reason for the argument. Mike had resisted telling Peter about us for almost two years. I knew Mike had made a poor choice in going to visit him. He had remained sober since his release from the substance abuse jail program until he visited with his brother. He knew Peter was on a drinking binge. Former alcoholics in sobriety know that they cannot be around other alcoholics. The temptation to consume alcohol is too great.

Mike was on a great path and had made a new beginning. He even went to his court-appointed therapist, Casey, regularly. Yet whenever Peter called, Mike did whatever he asked. Why didn't Mike say no to the temptation? My guess was that he was hungry for the closeness and the bond with his brother, no matter how flawed it was. Mike was a great man who at times made bad choices.

When I arrived at Mike's room, my feet still sandy from the beach, we sat on the love seat and talked for hours as the afternoon blurred into the night. I poured my love and comfort as best as I could into his heartbroken soul. I felt his pain and wanted to magically erase it somehow. I knew he needed a good listener. I stayed with him throughout the night, sleeping in the double bed next to his bed in the hotel room.

Over the next couple of days, I conveyed my sincere sorrow about having let him down by withdrawing money without his knowledge while he was in jail. I pointed out to him that he had made false promises regarding the money. Additionally, I spoke honestly about the promise he had made with the beachfront condo on which I had signed a lease but that he had never followed through on. He realized that we were both wrong, but it took him a while to get over it. I asked him for his forgiveness and told him I would never disappoint him in that way again. He accepted my apology.

My desire was to rebuild trust with him. Because of Mike's upbringing and his never having had a solid foundation, he had a hard time trusting people in general. I knew that deep down I was trustworthy. I am human and made a bad choice in withholding information about the money offered to me. Even though we had prior joint accounts, I should have sought his permission before withdrawing the money. I had tried to stay afloat financially, afraid of not having enough money. Fear drove my poor decision making. Also, I had trusted our neighbors' advice about waiting until Mike was out of jail to tell him, instead of trusting in God. I now know with all of my heart to trust in God. God will provide for all of my needs, including my financial ones. As a child of God, I know He has my best interest at heart.

Before we knew it, Mike and I had fallen deeply in love again. I slept at the hotel several nights a week even though I still lived at Diane's. Diane told me I had a glow about me and that I looked happy. Of course I was happy: our long days apart had ended. My suffering was over. I was reunited with the man I loved.

Mike shared with me his new dream of starting a Christian nonprofit for teens. His vision included bringing in semiprofessional athletes to offer basketball, baseball, and football clinics, with the intention of bringing local youth into a relationship with Christ.

With my past experience of being self-employed, coupled with having written a business plan, I began to structure his vision.

Some of Mike's friends he had met in counseling and jail were also eager to be involved with the project. I felt his intense passion for his dream and was eager to be of support to him. What a beautiful dream God had placed in Mike's heart. Even his banker was supportive. We told the banker Mike's idea, and he came up with the name Extreme Esteem Building, which we thought was terrific. With Mike's background as a talented athlete combined with his desire to empower the youth in Christ, this dream was in alignment with God's will. Mike had found his purpose.

Not only did I want to be a part of Mike's dream, but I knew this new start would give him hope. Before his new dream, Mike identified himself as an alcoholic. His true identity was that he was a child of God. I knew he had seeds of greatness in him. He had a great destiny and a mission to motivate him. He had his challenges in that he needed to grow past the alcoholism and legal entanglements, but God had mighty plans for Mike, and I wanted him to experience new joy in life.

Mike knew I had worked with young people in dance in Rhode Island for twelve years before moving to Florida. He pondered adding dance classes for young girls, but we decided to start the nonprofit with boys in middle school and high school. I warned Mike that he needed to be sober 24/7 to run this program. Mike's stubborn streak ignored my advice. He believed he could handle his drinking while starting the nonprofit.

"I can handle my drinking" is the great lie that alcoholics believe as they deny their addiction.

Sadly, with the pain he carried from his father's death and his most recent argument with Peter, Mike's drinking escalated even with the promise of a new future. I woke up one morning in the hotel to find that his body had rejected the overload of beer from the night before. He had vomited and defecated on the hotel sheets, and I found him half passed out on the bathroom floor. I immediately turned to his friend Chris, whom I called from the hotel lobby downstairs. Chris, a former addict and a Tom Cruise lookalike, had met Mike in the substance abuse program the previous summer. Chris advised me to call 911 immediately. He added, "Mike may hate you now for calling the paramedics, but you are saving his life." When the paramedics and police arrived, Mike agreed to go to the hospital of his own accord.

As the paramedics wheeled Mike to the ambulance on a stretcher, he shot an angry look toward me. I knew that once he became sober, he would understand that I had had no choice but to take action. The decision to call 911 came from a loving place in me. We had a dream to build our nonprofit together, and I was prepared to fight for it.

After being taken to the emergency room, Mike was admitted to the hospital for alcohol detoxification. The doctor informed me that 50 percent of the patients admitted with blood alcohol levels as high as Mike's never recover and, sadly, die. Mike had built such a high tolerance to alcohol that the doctor was baffled that he could even have a coherent conversation with

Mike. His blood alcohol level was medically considered to induce coma or even cause death. I prayed
incessantly that through detoxification, he would
recover and heal.

Chris visited and offered support that Mike needed
and appreciated while hospitalized. I went to the hospital on my days off from work. I took naps with Mike
in his hospital bed. A couple of times the nurse allowed
me to stay past evening visiting hours, and Mike and I
would watch TV together. After the "banana bag" IVs
were inserted into Mike's arm, his nutritional deficien-
cies were remedied. I thanked God for answering my
prayers with Mike's recovery.

After Mike was released from the hospital, he
checked into a hotel near where I lived with Diane. On
Halloween, he decided he was tired of seeing me drive
my old car. He took me to a local car dealer and to
my surprise graciously gave me six thousand dollars
to lease a new car in my name. The payments were
affordable because of the generous deposit he put
down. He always wanted me to have the best. That
was his way of showing his love to me. No man had
ever given me so much. We weren't even married yet.

I hoped and prayed that Mike's faith and his new
mission of forming a Christian nonprofit would keep
him from lapsing back into alcoholism. Never having
had an addiction of any kind myself, I had a hard time
understanding why he needed to numb out so often.
Initially looking at his alcoholism only as a moral and
health issue, I didn't consider the physiological factors
or the fact of genetic predisposition. His father and
brother were both alcoholics. This was a lifestyle that

he knew well and was comfortable with. It was a constant battle for him to stay sober.

I tried never to judge him, but to remain compassionate at all times. I fell short of the mark during our arguments, when I expressed disapproval of how much he drank. Unfortunately, Mike succumbed to drinking again a week after he was released from the hospital. He wasn't drinking as heavily as before, but it was still very hard to comprehend how one could do this to one's body, mind, and soul.

I had trouble understanding why, if he was a true believer, he depended on the alcohol instead of on God. If one is not depending on God, one is depending on some vice to make it through the tough times, such as antidepressants, drugs or alcohol, food binging, and so on. Everyone's depending on someone or something to fill the holes inside. Only God's spirit can fill the holes, the old wounds of loss, hurt, and disappointment. God is the ultimate restorer of healing. Like many of us, Mike tried to immediately numb the pain from his father's death instead of waiting on God's timing for healing. Mike searched for relief, but the only relief he found was through alcohol. I knew he suffered from depression and that he needed more help than he was getting from his court-appointed therapist.

Having been through therapy myself, I believe that therapy is an incredibly helpful tool. God places helpful counselors in our lives. However, instead of having to wait years for change through weekly therapy sessions, the learning curve can be shortened. I've heard of testimonies where God has delivered addicts instantly. I prayed for Mike to be set free in this way from his bondage of addiction. Such an act required Mike to activate a key of faith for God's power to be unleashed.

The Bible clearly says, "Do not get drunk with wine . . . but be filled with the spirit" (Ephesians 5:18).

# 9

## tragedy Sets its Course

**November 2012**

Mike was arrested again for missing yet another court date. A couple of weeks later, he was released from jail. I was disappointed that we were not able to spend Thanksgiving together. However, I enjoyed a fun and festive dinner at Diane's home. After he was released from jail, Mike checked with his bank and saw that no money had been withdrawn from his checking account. I had promised him that I would never again withdraw such a large amount of money from his account without first talking to him.

One sunny morning, the doorbell rang. I was beyond surprised to find Mike standing on my doorstep. He had found his way back to me. Our eyes smiled as I felt joy rush inside of me. We kissed passionately and fell into each other's arms on my bed. Diane rented him a room for the week in her home where we lived. I wanted Mike by my side.

Before Mike's release from jail, Peter appeared on a talk show on television for his womanizing. Colleen,

Peter's current girlfriend, had informed me about the show and the date it would air. Diane and I watched the taped show together. Nothing I saw shocked me, for I had already lived through the web of lies in which Peter and I had ended our relationship.

Before arriving on the show, Peter had no idea which ex-girlfriend had invited him to be there. It was definitely not Colleen or myself. We both wondered who had asked Peter to be there. The producers strived to create an element of surprise and mystery. Peter was, no doubt, a modern "Don Juan" with his gorgeous appearance and charming influence over women. The show also arranged a taping in Peter's home.

Peter knew what to expect before arriving at the studio in Los Angeles. The host of the show basically warned women to stay away from men like Peter. Peter tried to laugh it off, but I knew him well enough to see that he was embarrassed. His charming smile hid the pain.

After the show was over, I thought to myself, *At times, I'm too trusting with people I don't know. Perhaps I'm naïve in some ways.* I was definitely guilty of trusting Peter too early without fully knowing him. However, Mike and I had built a solid foundation first. I knew that there had never been a true love connection between Peter and me, although we had been intensely infatuated with "falling in love." Peter once said to me, "I'm never letting you go back to Rhode Island." My deeper understanding made it clear that Peter was the catalyst in my transition to Florida. However, if I had not met Peter, I would never have met Mike, the love of my life. It had all been divinely ordered by God.

Colleen, who lived with Peter when he agreed to be on the show, was mortified that he would reveal this side of himself on national television. She begged and pleaded with him not to do the show. She was justifiably concerned what her family and friends would think if they saw Peter on the show. I originally thought to myself, *Perhaps Peter is trying to change the way he treats women.*

However, after I watched the show, I saw that he had no remorse for the false promises that he had made to women, including me. I later learned from Colleen that Peter's hope was to be "discovered" for his "five minutes of fame." After the show finished taping, Peter flew back to his home in Boca Raton where he and Colleen continued to live together.

My sister, who was visiting with my mother in Pennsylvania, called to say, "We just watched Peter on television."

"You've got to be kidding," I responded in disbelief. My sister, who never watches daytime television, had happened to walk past the television on that particular day. She confidently told my mother that she knew it was Peter on the show. My sister had met Peter during the summer I lived with him when I first moved to Florida. Even though I was obviously no longer with him, I couldn't believe the coincidence that my family had seen, firsthand, Peter's confessing on national television that he mistreated women.

Although Mike initially missed the show, he watched a taped version later on a DVD that his mother had mailed to him. He couldn't understand why Peter had put himself through the humiliation. "What in the world was Peter thinking by going on that show?" he said. Mike became somewhat obsessive, watching the DVD repeatedly and trying to make sense of it all.

## December 2012

Then the worst possible event occurred, one that none of us anticipated. Peter committed suicide by plunging a knife into his neck. Colleen found him lying dead on the kitchen floor after she awakened early in the morning. She immediately ran across the street to the neighbors for help. When the detectives and police arrived on the scene, Colleen was questioned for approximately three hours before Detective Miller called Mike with the horrendous news. We were all united in shock.

Upon learning what had happened, Mike became so distraught that he punched a hole in my bedroom door with his bare fist and immediately went into denial. "No, no, no, this cannot be true," he wailed. "No way is this true."

"Mike, I'm sorry," I said. "I'm so sorry. I love you, and we are going to get through this together." I didn't know the appropriate words to use to respond to this tragedy. I took a deep breath as I tried to get clear headed. I then calmly proceeded, "We need to get ready and go up to the house immediately. The detectives are waiting for us." Even though God has gifted me with remaining calm under pressure, I moved slowly getting us out the door. It takes me forever to finish getting ready to go out the door on a normal day, but with the heavy emotional toll, I moved at the speed of molasses.

Peter's sudden death was a shock and surprise to us all. There was no suicide note. It was all quite strange in that it was an uncommon method by which to end one's life.

I drove Mike to Peter's house. After driving for close to a half hour, we arrived and faced a new obstacle: we were unable to get past the security gate. Mike's name had been blackballed from the list of guests at the gate ever since he and Peter had argued on the day I had rushed off the beach with my sandy feet to help him.

I called Colleen on my cell phone. "Colleen, we are here at the gate and they won't let us through. Mike is getting really upset and angry about it." The police officer at Peter's house drove to the gate to tell the security officer to let us into the house.

Peter's body had already been removed. It had been sent to the morgue for an autopsy, but a pool of blood remained on the kitchen floor. Mike's initial reaction upon walking into Peter's house was anger followed by shock. He sat on top of the granite bar and stared at the pool of blood for hours. As morbid as it may sound, I couldn't get him to move from the spot of the suicide.

"Mike, please come sit out in the lanai with Colleen and me," I pleaded. "It's not good for you to keep sitting there. Please, Mike." He wouldn't budge. He wouldn't talk to Colleen or to me. He remained silent.

Having been grilled by the police for three hours before our arrival, Colleen was distraught beyond words. She had already made calls to the family and to

Peter's friends. I asked her how I could help with phone calls. Detective Miller had also been extremely helpful and handed me both her business card and a card for a professional cleaning-and-restoration company.

I had to make the call to the restoration company for the blood to be cleaned from the kitchen floor and lower walls. I had to be strong for both Mike and Colleen. I also knew that my strength came from God. I had never been through anything like this in my life. It was intensely sad and surreal. I walked through the motions as if I were in some strange dream.

Mike and I slept at Peter's home that evening. Colleen gave me clean sheets to make the bed. It was after midnight when we turned in and tried with great difficulty to sleep. Mike and I held each other closely as I reminded him, "I love you, Mike, with all of my heart. I'm right here by your side, always." Somehow, despite the intensity, we drifted to sleep.

Before that evening, Mike numbed himself emotionally with any alcohol he could find in the house. Mike's tender heart grieved intensely. The first night of loss is always the most raw. I, too, had a particularly hard time. Not only did I empathize with Mike's profound sadness and loss, but I had to deal with my memories of Peter too.

The memories arose from living in the house with Peter for two and a half months. Various memories flashed in my mind of how we had lived together "once upon a time." I pressed heavily into prayer that evening. I asked God for strength and comfort for both Mike and myself. I prayed that God would heal Michael's broken heart and cover him like a blanket of comfort during the night.

The next day, I told Colleen, "When Mike wakes up, please make sure he knows that I'll be back in a few hours. Otherwise he'll be confused about why I'm not here in the house." I drove back to our home in Fort Lauderdale, took a shower, and gathered some clothing. After I packed a little clothing for Mike and me, I was driving back to Peter's house to be with Mike and Colleen when I received a strange phone call.

"Where are you?" a woman demanded.

Not recognizing the voice, I asked, "Who is this?"

It was Mike's aunt. I told her, "I'm in the car and I'll be there in approximately fifteen minutes."

I was shocked and angry that she spoke to me in that tone. After all, I had helped out as best I could the day before by comforting Mike and Colleen. I didn't have to answer to her. She was inconsiderate in the way she approached me on the phone, particularly given the sensitive circumstances surrounding Peter's death.

I arrived at Peter's house to witness another horrible scene. When I walked through the front door, there was an uncomfortable tension in the air. I was introduced to Mike's mother and her two sisters who sat at the bar off of the formal living room. At first, I didn't recognize Mike's aunt, whom I had met in the past and who now sat on a bar stool smacking her chewing gum. Cold and distant, her demeanor had changed dramatically from when I first remembered her.

Mike had lost his brother, whom he loved deeply, the previous day. Poor Mike was being criticized by his family for his drinking, when he desperately needed love and comfort in that moment. After witnessing the cold criticism from Mike's mother and aunts, I softened my view toward Peter and his problems with women. I felt a new compassion toward Peter, not only because of the suicide, but because the two brothers had endured such a painful childhood.

Next, his mother and her two sisters criticized me with their verbal attacks. They wanted to know why I had dated Peter first and then Michael. I don't remember their words verbatim, but I do remember how they made me feel: like I was on trial and had to prove myself. I couldn't believe the coldness and evil I was witnessing. I had had enough of their disrespect, and told them point-blank, "There has been a death, and we should be here to comfort and support one another." I then said firmly, "You ladies have a good day. I'm done talking with you." I felt bad about leaving Mike alone inside with the wolves but departed quickly to sit with Colleen on the lanai facing the pool.

As we sat together, Colleen shared with me that Peter and Mike's mother and aunts had told her earlier, "This is a family discussion." They had shunned her from their conversation, which was indicative of their coldness. Obviously, Colleen was intensely sad after losing Peter. As we talked, she chain-smoked, and her cigarette butts overflowed the dirty ashtray. Her poor delicate hands shook as she drank her Coca-Cola and repeatedly swallowed aspirin.

Mike's mother and aunts finally left us in peace. I offered to bring back dinner so we could get some food and nourishment into us.

The next morning, Mike's mother and his aunt arrived at the security gate. Colleen, Mike, and I had agreed that after the previous day's fiasco, we were not comfortable in their presence. None of us wanted a repeat of the horrible manner in which his family had acted the day before. However, his mother was in tears at the gate when she found out Mike had banned her from the house.

Mike and Colleen walked together to the gate. I felt protective about him since I knew he was vulnerable. His mother claimed that she needed Peter's Social Security number for identification at the morgue; I knew she could have easily gotten it over the phone.

After seeing his mother in tears, Mike let her back into the house. Colleen and his mother went into Peter's office while Mike disappeared. His aunt walked into the house once her car was admitted through the gate. Once inside, his mother and aunt claimed they needed an urn for Peter's ashes. After looking around the office, they took an expensive, autographed basketball and football without even talking to Michael. Colleen said, "I don't think that's what Peter wanted."

Mike's aunt retorted, "You have no rights here" as they closed the front door and left.

Mike came back from his walk. I asked him, "Why weren't you here protecting the house?"

"I needed to walk and get some fresh air," he replied.

I later realized that after the way his family had treated him the day before, I couldn't blame him for not wanting to be around that negativity two days in a row.

Colleen explained to Mike what had occurred with Peter's sports memorabilia. Several hours later, Mike called and left a voice mail on his mom's cell phone. He informed her that he had called the police and reported the sports memorabilia stolen. In reality, he never actually called the police.

Mike compared his mom and aunt to "looters in a store with free access." He said, "They acted like cheap thieves, grabbing what they could get on their way out the door." In addition to dealing with the anger over his brother's death, this act infuriated him even more. Mike knew that Peter's belongings should have been discussed openly with him, as neither of the brothers had any real relationship with their mother whatsoever. It utterly shocked me that a family could behave this way with one another after a tragic death.

I had originally met his aunt at her church in Fort Lauderdale several months earlier—the same church where I had dropped Mike off that rainy night when we had miraculously crossed paths for the second time after Mike's release from the substance abuse program. Thanks to God's intervention, we had learned then that we were neighbors.

His aunt had initially appeared warm and friendly. I had attended a service at the church, where she was a greeter when she wasn't managing the church office. The second time I saw her was when Mike and I went to visit her at the church office one day. Mike gave her a gift card for groceries that he was donating to those in the church who were in need of food. Even with all the legal problems Mike was facing at the time, he never stopped caring for the oppressed.

By the third day after Peter's death, the family had left. The first of Peter's friends to arrive after hearing the news was Cindy. Cindy loved Peter as a friend and took care of his plants and errands every Thursday like clockwork. After Cindy arrived, Colleen pried open a locked black filing cabinet in Peter's office. Cindy watched closely over Colleen, feeling the need to protect Peter's belongings. Cindy handed Mike the valuables inside, including some antique Chinese money.

Later that afternoon Cort, an old friend of both Mike and Peter's, arrived to give his condolences. Cindy informed Mike and Cort that Peter had told her several times that he had wanted Colleen out of the house for months, but she would not leave. The next door neighbor, Jack, with whom Mike and I conversed in the driveway, also offered his condolences and confirmed what Cindy had said about Peter wanting Colleen to leave.

We also learned that there had been a domestic dispute and the police had been called to the house several months before Peter's death. Apparently, during an argument Colleen or Peter had thrown patio furniture against the sliding glass door that separated the house from the lanai. We noticed that the glass door was off the track and needed to be fixed. What were we to think?

Next, we were shocked to learn that a few of Peter's friends suspected that Colleen might have killed him. Questions arose about whether Peter's death was a homicide or a suicide. None of his close friends believed Peter had taken his own life. One friend said, "He was too full of himself." Mike and I talked about their serious accusations for a while. As horrible as Peter's death was, we believed he had taken his own life.

However, Cort had a considerable influence over Mike's decision making. Cort and Mike discussed what to do about Colleen living in the house. Cort shared with Mike and me his first impression of Colleen. "She's a hustler," he said. After Mike and Cort talked for a while, Cort told Colleen it would be best for everyone if she left the house that evening.

It certainly wasn't healthy for Colleen to be living in the house where she had found Peter's body. However, she needed some time to recoup and recover from the trauma. Decisions were made quickly. Cort made arrangements for Peter's Mercedes to be returned to the car dealer that same day. He aggressively made decisions and called the shots. I realized that Cort was acting on his instincts to protect Mike and thus, Peter's home. Unfortunately, Mike was unable to take charge because of his state of mind.

Colleen packed her suitcases and golf clubs, and I drove her to a car-rental agency that evening. I said to her, "I am sorry that this is happening to you." I felt sympathy toward her. She had just lost the man she loved. She now faced a long drive from Florida to New Jersey, taking Peter's dog, Kahlua, with her.

More of Peter's friends came forward saying they believed his death had been a homicide. I never believed that Colleen was capable of such a hor-rific act of violence. We would have to wait for the autopsy results and the investigation to be over to have our answer.

# 10

## How Do You Mend a Broken Heart?

❧❧❧

U.S. Census data from 2015 shows that thirty thousand people every year commit suicide and that one person attempts suicide every minute in America.

Life is a gift from God. Those who commit suicide take the life God has given them and destroy it. Suicide is an expression of self-hatred and of selfishness. Suicide is a sin, although a pardonable, forgivable sin.

The one who takes his or her own life is unable to see all the shattered pieces they leave behind. Brokenness and destruction had set in more deeply with Mike. I felt led to guide him closer to God during his grieving, for **God promises comfort** and healing in our difficulties. "Who comforts us in all our tribulation, that we may be able to comfort those who are in any trouble, with the comfort with which we ourselves are comforted by God" (2 Corinthians 1:4).

I knew that both my and Mike's source of strength was derived from God's Word and prayers for healing. No human healing can come remotely close to God's healing. Mike was mourning his father's death, and his brother's suicide only compounded his grieving.

I asked him one morning, "Would you trust in God to help you heal?"

"I'm angry with God right now for taking Peter away," he said.

"Mike, God didn't take Peter away. We have free choice every day. Peter's choice to end his life was not in alignment with God's will. Only God determines when our last breath and day will be."

Although I guided Mike into pressing into God for comfort and healing, Mike seemed interested only in self-medicating through alcohol. Peter had to have known that his suicide would break Mike's heart. Peter had witnessed Mike's falling to pieces in reaction to the death of their father.

Mike's dream of a Christian nonprofit for youth was obviously placed on the back burner. He needed to heal first. Mike was suffering from a broken heart. His beautiful, pure heart, which I loved, was broken. I know that God is in the business of restoring brokenness. I prayed for Mike's healing and restoration.

Mike asked me to move into his brother's home with him in Boca Raton, where, ironically I had lived when I first moved to Florida to be with Peter. As awkward as it seemed at first, I knew he needed my support and love as he grieved deeply over Peter's death.

After I spoke to Diane about Mike's circumstances, she understood I would no longer be renting from her. I packed my belongings and left my home in Fort Lauderdale to move back to Peter's house with Mike.

It certainly didn't help matters that Christmas was less than a few weeks away. I tried to decorate the house with a few Christmas decorations I had found in the garage. There were several nights when Mike cried as he put his head on my shoulder. How I wished I could erase his pain. I had never known any man who suffered the degree of pain he did. I had also never known any man's heart as large as Mike's.

Mike knew I loved Christmas. Although he dealt with the intense pain of his circumstances, he wanted to create a special Christmas for me by placing my needs above his own. On Christmas Day, we called my mom to wish her a Merry Christmas. Mike had a great rapport with her. "Hi, Mom," he said. "Merry Christmas. I want you to know that I intend to marry your daughter as soon as everything settles with my brother's death." My mom already knew how much we loved each other. She was genuinely happy for both of us. Mike also commented to me that South Florida was not a wholesome place to live. He had a dream for us to move to Austin, Texas, to be near his father's side of the family.

Mike took me to the Carolina Club for a special Christmas dinner. The country club was where he and his father used to golf together. He had taken me there once before for dinner. I have fond memories of us walking the greens where he and his dad used to golf. We walked in the wet dew of the grass at night. Mike said, "Karen, we aren't supposed to walk the golf course at night, but I wanted to show you where I loved spending time with my dad."

Not only did Mike's drinking steadily increase, but a new pattern emerged in that his food consumption dwindled after Peter's death. A lack of appetite is common for one who is grieving, but Mike pushed dangerous boundaries, taking in little to no food daily. I knew I needed to get him help for his depression. I found a Christian minister who specialized in grieving. He didn't even charge a fee. I called and made an appointment for Mike.

The day of the appointment Mike announced, "I'm not going. I don't feel up to it."

"Mike, we need to go right now," I replied. "This minister has generously taken time out of his day to meet with us. Please, let's go!" But he refused. I was disappointed that my efforts were going nowhere. Perhaps he was not ready to open up and share his feelings of pain yet.

Mike had said occasionally to me in his deep pain and mourning, "I wish God would take me from this earth, but I am not that lucky." When I initially heard that, I felt it was the alcohol talking, as alcoholics tend to have a self-pitying, "poor me" mentality when under the influence of alcohol. However, after Mike repeated this comment a couple of times, I knew his depression had deepened. Mike needed help. He also made the comment, "I'm doing the same thing my brother did. I'm just doing it more slowly."

In my attempt to make sense of it all, I responded, "If you are going to leave this earth, you're taking me with you. You're not leaving me behind. You see how your father's and brother's deaths have caused you deep pain. Is that what you want me to go through? I don't want to be here without you. You're my other half."

"You'll be fine," Mike replied, in denial of the truth I had spoken.

I immediately called a local mental health facility to explain that my fiancé had expressed thoughts of suicide. They sent a mental health counselor directly to the house fairly quickly. When the young man appeared at the door, I felt grateful that Mike would have the help he desperately needed. In the past, he had refused my suggestions to meet with grief counselors. This idea worked better, and having a counselor come directly to our home was a great alternative.

However, Mike, in a private conversation (which I overheard in the dining room) said to the counselor, "I'm not suicidal. I just have a drinking problem." He continued his lie. "I'm in the process of getting help. I'm looking for a detox facility."

As I walked privately with the counselor to his car in the driveway, I told him adamantly, "Mike is desperately in need of help. I'm concerned that his life is in danger."

"I can only make an assessment based on what Mike has told me," the counselor explained. "He knows his next step is to get treatment for his alcoholism."

I thanked the young man for his time and visit. However, I felt devastated that no progress had been made. I was frustrated that Mike had fooled the counselor into believing that he was not suicidal. I felt like I was racing against the clock for help. I knew Mike couldn't keep living in his destructive condition.

Next, we were shocked to learn that Mike's mother wasn't planning a funeral for Peter. She told Mike one night on the phone, "I take comfort in the fact that Peter was saved through confirmation as a teen. He's already in heaven." She didn't feel a funeral was necessary and had had him cremated. Although Peter had shared with Colleen and a few friends on occasion that he had created a will, his expressed wishes for a burial never happened. A week after Peter's death, Mike and I searched through every file in his office. We found nothing. Peter's will was never found.

At the end of the phone call, Mike pleaded, "Mom, I want a portion of Peter's ashes."

"Mike, I've already made the decision to keep Peter's ashes," his mother replied. Her refusal to divide the ashes caused Mike more anguish and pain. She had no regard for his feelings even though he was the closest family member to Peter. She was well aware of her rights as next of kin under Florida state law to do as she pleased.

One night, Mike and I went grocery shopping. Upon leaving the grocery store, I noticed him walking with a strange gait as he pushed the shopping cart toward the car. His legs stiffened as he leaned backward like a toy soldier. He lost consciousness and dropped quickly to the ground. A witness in the parking lot who saw Mike fall called 911. The paramedics arrived within minutes. As Mike regained consciousness, he refused to be driven to the hospital. All of his vital signs checked out okay when he was assessed in the ambulance. I knew that his lack of eating along with the stress from grieving had resulted in his unconsciousness.

I offered a way to help relieve some of his stress. "Mike, would you be open to the idea of getting a professional massage?" I asked him.

"No thanks, I'm not interested in a massage," he replied.

I decided I was in need of a massage, given the daily stress I was under. Mike came with me to my appointment and waited in the car while I had my massage. It was a mistake on my part; he should have stayed home. With his depression, though, I tried to get him out of the house as much as I could.

As the massage therapist started to work on my upper shoulders, I slowly felt my body melt into relaxation. Then I heard someone knocking loudly on the glass door of the outside entrance. I asked myself, *Could that be Mike knocking?* A few moments later, the loud banging on the door increased.

I said to the massage therapist, "I don't mind if you need to stop the session and go check the front door. It sounds pretty urgent."

The knocking came from an ambulance driver, who was trying to find me. Evidently, Mike had knocked at the door the first time in an attempt to find me. I felt terrible that Mike had panicked when he couldn't find me and dropped, unconscious, to the ground, similar to the grocery store incident.

I frantically rushed out the glass door to find Mike in an ambulance in the parking lot. An older man with a gray beard had witnessed Mike's fall and called the paramedics. Mike had hit his cheek hard on the pavement. The side of his face was scraped and bloody. People were gathered around the ambulance. The paramedics drove Mike to a local hospital, and I followed behind in my car. Upon arrival at the emergency room, Mike was immediately treated. Luckily, he didn't need any stitches. He did, however, have to wear a patch over his cheek. Hours later, after I had waited in the emergency room, he was released. "Mike, I was so worried about you. I'm glad you're okay. We can go home now," I said in relief and gratitude.

A couple of weeks later, Miriam, our cleaning lady, arrived at the house. An astonishing event took place that day that I would never have imagined in my wildest thoughts. However, as mysterious and unexpected as it was, the circumstances of that day led to a more peaceful way of life for Mike and me, thanks to God sending "His angel of light."

Miriam gathered her usual cleaning supplies in preparation of cleaning the bathroom first. She glanced my way and saw sadness in my eyes and countenance. "Is everything okay, Miss Karen?" she asked in her distinctive Brazilian accent.

"No. I guess you can see it in my face. It is horrible, what I'm dealing with in terms of Mike's brokenness and grieving." I continued, "We argue way too much because of Mike's alcoholism as I try to balance the challenges of daily life. Mike has resisted all of my efforts to help him with his depression and grieving. He criticizes me on occasion in ways that he would never say when he was sober," I confessed. "He tells me that I'm not as organized and efficient as I think I am. He tells me that my job of running the front of a restaurant as head hostess is a joke, given that I'm college educated. His words hurt me at times."

She reminded me that it was not Mike, but the Enemy attacking me through Mike's words. The Enemy, Satan, had a stranglehold on Mike through his alcohol addiction.

She guided me to the sofa so we could sit down and talk. She said, "I knew before I came here today that I was sent here to help you and Mike. I didn't really come here to clean today." Initially, I looked perplexed, but then I understood that God had sent His "angel" to help with our situation.

Miriam asked that I get a Bible to get started. We called Mike into the living room to sit with us. He and I sat next to each other on the tan leather sofa. "Miriam is here to help us, Mike," I said in an upbeat tone. Unsure of how Mike would respond, I was pleasantly surprised when he agreed to listen to whatever Miriam had to say. Mike had drunk vodka earlier in the day and was under the influence. Miriam stood at the end of the sofa reading to us from the Bible.

Next, Miriam went over to where Mike sat and stood behind him, placing her small hands on his head in prayer. "I rebuke you, Satan. You have no rights here. Leave. I rebuke you," Miriam commanded repeatedly. She commanded the demonic spirits oppressing Mike to leave. These demonic spirits entered through the gateways of alcohol and anger. Within a minute of her most fervent prayer, Mike slipped into unconsciousness with her hands still on his head. God's miraculous hand was at work when Miriam confirmed, "Let

Mike rest. God heals and restores through sleep." I had witnessed firsthand God's power.

I felt a huge sense of relief come over my body. I talked more with Miriam, because I needed to process the miracle I had witnessed. When Mike woke up approximately thirty minutes later, he wept uncontrollably.

After he woke up, Mike's face astonished me. His countenance looked like that of a brand new baby. I was elated, and ran to get my camera to capture the experience. I took pictures of Miriam and Mike together and one of Mike alone. He looked humble with no apparent signs of anger in his demeanor. Additionally, it had been a dark, cloudy day earlier when Miriam had first arrived, but after Mike woke up, rays of sunlight beamed into our home.

Mike had been set free from his addiction. I had prayed in the past for him to be set free instantly. God had answered my prayer in His timing. Although Mike had been angry with God for Peter's death, God's unconditional love never wavered from Mike.

I had never witnessed anything remotely close to what took place through that powerful prayer with Miriam's healing hands. I had trouble comprehending the miracle that had taken place right in our home. Miriam explained, "It is the power of God working through me. My dad had the same gift of healing hands as I do."

She further explained, "I knew that I had the anointing of God upon me throughout this prayer of deliverance and healing." Miriam allowed herself to be used as a vessel for God to work through her. I will never forget that miracle as long as I live. Mike was finally free. The words to the well-known doxology ran through my head: "Praise God from whom all blessings flow!"

# 11

## Your Honor, May I Speak?

**March 2013**

L ife appeared great. Mike's legal entanglement with
the court system was almost over. The only requirement left was for him to show up at his monthly probation appointments. Probation required him to stay
sober and seek employment. With the money Mike had
inherited from his father's properties, including a home
in Austin, Texas, he really didn't care about meeting the
probation's goal of employment. It appeared he was
off to a good start when he completed his first probation appointment.

Although legally the light appeared at the end of
the tunnel, sadly, Mike's personal battle with alcoholism reared its ugly head again. His drinking was
spurred when we received the autopsy results from
Peter's death. We received a call from the detective

on the case who confirmed the coroner's report that Peter's death was indeed a suicide.

Peter's death was not a homicide as several of his friends had suspected. Despite the controversy, I had always believed it was a suicide. Because there was never a suicide note, we would never have our answer to why Peter had taken his life, but I suspected that his suffering from bipolar disorder, combined with his bankruptcy, played a major role. Peter had struggled financially for the last few years before his death.

Mike didn't handle the news very well. Once again he clung to alcohol to cope. In addition to the autopsy results, being in Peter's home was a major hindrance to Mike's sobriety, because he was constantly reminded of his brother's death. It was heart wrenching to witness the pain Mike suffered from the loss of his brother as well as his father. I desired on a deep level for him to know and feel my love.

Sadly, the majority of Mike's friends never called to offer support after Peter's death. A few friends called him only because they knew that his pure heart would help them financially. Not only does a crisis reveal one's character, but death reveals one's character as well.

However, Mike had two friends who remained loyal to him without any ulterior motives of financial profit. One friend, also named Mike, cut our hair every six weeks. He checked in on Mike regularly to make sure he was okay. The second friend was Christian. Christian was a special friend completely unlike the others and always found time to spend with Mike on the phone during his initial grieving. Mike had met and connected with Christian at the gym after he'd completed his substance abuse program. After Peter's death, Christian's genuine love for Jesus and strong faith guided Mike to hope and light many times.

It must have grieved God's heart to see one of His children set free from addiction as Mike had been, only to fall back into the destructive pattern of drinking. God gave Mike chance after chance with new beginnings, first through the substance abuse program in lieu of jail time and then through His miracle of deliverance via Miriam. Mike should have entered an alcohol rehabilitation center after God lovingly freed him from his addiction. The battle of sobriety required that Mike commit to the path.

**God's promise of His presence** in Mike's life was evident. God continued to show His unconditional love to Mike even when Mike had strayed from God.

I have no clue how Mike went a year with barely any food, and with alcohol poisoning his body and mind. He lived day after day, his only calories coming from alcohol. It is physically impossible to live that amount of time without any substantial food. God's grace kept him alive more than humanly possible in miraculous ways. I witnessed firsthand God's unconditional love for Michael in the supernatural way in which He kept him alive.

**God created us to reveal His unconditional love to us.** "And we have known and believed the love that God has for us. God is love, and he who abides in love abides in God, and God in him" (1 John 4:16).

Once, I boldly proclaimed, "Mike, do you know how much God loves you? It is a miracle that you are alive after all these months of drinking alcohol with no real food."

I pressed more deeply. "God gave you a special heart for a reason, Mike. He wants you alive. God has a purpose for your life. What about the dream God placed in your heart to lead teenage boys into a relationship with Christ through a sports clinic?" I paused, and then continued, "I know you need to heal first from your grieving before undertaking such a project. Remember, you have a purpose to live for. God's fighting for your life as I am."

Once again, Mike's drinking binge perpetuated a cycle of missed probation appointments. He didn't want the probation officer to see him drunk. He knew the only acceptable excuse for missing his appointment was being hospitalized. Hospitalization equaled sobriety in my book.

"Either you can go to jail again if you miss your probation appointment or you can go to the hospital and sober up. The choice is yours," I firmly explained.

"Will you make the call to the paramedics for me?" Mike asked. Within minutes, an ambulance had arrived in our driveway and taken him to the emergency room at the local hospital.

Mike arrived at the emergency room with an alcohol level of .425. The doctors were once again baffled by how he maintained a coherent conversation with them. Any blood alcohol level of over .400 is considered to be coma or death by all medical accounts. Michael mystified the doctors as a walking marvel for having built up such a high tolerance for alcohol. After he became sober, his hospital tests showed that his potassium levels were dangerously low. He received IVs to sustain and nourish him, because he was severely malnourished from lack of food.

Meanwhile, Mike's probation officer called me to find out why Mike had missed his appointment. I explained that he had been hospitalized for alcoholism. The officer drove to the hospital to verify the facts I had discussed with him. Mike's choice of getting treatment for his alcoholism saved him from going back to jail for missing his probation appointment. His doctor at the hospital informed the probation officer that Mike had almost died and that his alcohol levels were off the chart.

A month later, Mike once again purposely missed his probation appointment. The doorbell rang. I had just gotten out of the shower, my hair was wet, and I was wearing a soft pink bathrobe when I answered the door. The probation officer and three other officers in bulletproof vests entered the foyer. I went into the master bedroom and announced, "Mike, your probation officer is here for you."

They arrested and handcuffed Mike immediately for violating his probation. My eyes welled up with tears as I bent down to put his socks and sneakers on him. As Mike and the probation officer walked toward the front door, Mike said, "She needs to leave as well."

The officer, who could smell the alcohol on him, ignored Mike's request and said calmly, "She's done nothing wrong. Let's go, Mike."

Out the door they went. At first, I felt hurt that Mike had told the officer to ask me to leave the house when I had done nothing wrong. However, I had to remind myself that Mike had trust issues, especially when he was under the influence of alcohol. Perhaps he was afraid that when he returned from jail, the house would be empty of its contents. He was unable to understand that my deepest desire was to build trust and remain with him because I loved him.

Mike had always been there for me as my protector. If anyone insulted me or even glared at me the wrong way, they'd had to deal with Mike. He had a fierce, natural instinct to protect me like no one else. Sadly, over time his mental processing became paranoid and off kilter from alcoholism and malnutrition.

One cannot think that one can escape the effects of drinking a half gallon of vodka every other day with little to no food and that all will be fine. It is a fact that alcohol abuse destroys the brain cells and that functioning and memory become impaired. Combine alcohol abuse with the fact that Mike ate little to no food daily for months, and damage to the brain was inevitable. Many alcoholics believe that they are impervious to this brain dysfunction, but believe me, this is a real fact that I witnessed firsthand. I don't need a medical degree to understand it. Alcoholism is extremely destructive to the mind and body.

After Mike was arrested in our home, he served a few weeks in jail for having missed his probation appointment. I prayed for his release from jail. I awaited a court date and finally received notice of the date he was set to go before the judge.

I found my way to the courthouse and sat on the wooden bench in the courtroom. I anxiously tapped my foot on the floor as I waited to see Mike enter the room. Mike came through a back door with the other prisoners from jail, his hands and feet shackled as he waited to go before the judge. He sat with the other convicts. It sickened me to see him like this in a courtroom. Inside, I boiled with feelings of injustice. Mike was neither a drug dealer nor a drug addict, yet he was chained in court as a common criminal. Alcoholism had affected his brain chemistry, leading to bad judgment and bad decisions such as missing his probation appointments.

His eyes scanned the courtroom in hopes of finding me. When our eyes met, I smiled slightly as I tried to remain strong and supportive. Finally, after three terribly long hours of waiting for Mike's name to be called, his case went before the judge. He had a public defender represent him at that point.

Next, I silently asked God for the courage to ask the judge if I could speak on Mike's behalf before the court. I was granted permission. I stood and pleaded with the judge that the truth needed to be told about Michael. I said with confidence to the judge and prosecuting attorney, "The truth is that Michael does not have a drug problem. He has an alcohol problem. He's an alcoholic."

"What is your relationship to the defendant?" the judge inquired.

"I am his fiancée," I answered.

Next, the judge read out loud to the court the probation officer's report that Mike had nearly died from alcoholism after he was admitted to a local hospital. The judge concluded by speaking to the state prosecutor and courtroom. She said she had decided to drop the case based on the probation officer's report and the fact that Mike's case had lingered too long. I believe that my testimony in court about Mike's alcoholism also strengthened her resolve with his case.

Mike no longer needed to report to probation. I witnessed God's work once again. God had answered my prayers. Mike was given a new chance to start life again. The horrible pressure of jail and probation, and of being falsely accused of drug usage, was finally over, as the case had been dropped once and for all.

Thanks to God's mercy and love, Mike's case finished victoriously. God's plan saved Mike's life as jail forced his sobriety again. Additionally, I thanked God for the timing of Mike's sobriety in jail, because my mother and uncle were to visit the following week and had no inkling about what Mike and I had endured. Spring was in the air as new life and hope abounded.

# 12

## *Ashes for Beauty*

❦

**May 2013**

"Are you ready, Mike?" I asked. "Let's go pick up my mom and uncle. You will also meet my sister for the first time." We flew down the highway and made record time: I didn't want to be late to pick up my family. They had spent the first week at my sister's home in Palm Beach Gardens and planned to spend the second week with Mike and me in Boca Raton.

I cannot deny that I was slightly apprehensive about whether Mike would drink alcohol around my family, since he had returned to drinking after his release from jail, although not as heavily as before. As elated as I was that Mike's legal problems were now a memory of the past, he still hadn't healed in regard to his brother's death. Mike's behavior was at times unpredictable. However, I knew how much he loved being with people. He was truly as excited as I was about having my family with us in our home. I sensed Mike's hunger to have family around.

One evening before dinner, Mike and I drove my family to the beach that I loved and where we often dined at a special restaurant overlooking the ocean. My family, Mike, and I walked along the beach where the palm trees framed the paved sidewalk.

The next morning, Mike picked up eggs, bacon, and cheese to make breakfast for everyone. After he returned from his errands, he headed straight to my mom, who sat on the sofa, and surprised her with a beautiful tennis bracelet. When my mother opened her gift, she was stunned. She said, "Oh, Mike, this is beautiful, but I cannot accept it." She, of course, did eventually accept his generous gift.

Those days with Mike and my family together were special. After a three-night stay, we drove them back and hugged and kissed one another goodbye. Toward the end of my family's visit Mike said, "I would love for your family to stay forever. I wish they didn't have to leave."

I replied, "I will always cherish their visit too. Wow, seeing you enjoying yourself in their company was great. Thank you for treating my family to dinner every night. Your kind heart never ceases to amaze me, Mike."

Despite Mike's grieving, he tried his best to create a better life for us. He and I enjoyed our time together while living in his brother's glamorous house. I grew to love living in Peter's palace of a home. It was our home, and for the most part, we were happy there. We went out to dinner a few nights a week. Mike always let me choose the restaurant.

I enjoyed the visits from Miriam, our cleaning lady, who prayed with us before she cleaned our home.

Miriam reminded us, "Mike and Karen, when temptations come, run to the Word of God." She continued, "Just as our bodies need food for nourishment, our spirits need nourishment from scripture."

Miriam eventually caught on that Mike had returned to drinking when she saw empty vodka bottles as she cleaned the kitchen. She seemed disappointed that Mike had caved in to the temptation of drinking again after God had miraculously delivered him from his alcohol addiction through her prayer. She never judged him, though. She saw the goodness and love in Mike despite his struggle with alcoholism.

Mike and I frequently shopped at the mall in Boca Raton, which was lined with high-end boutiques like Louis Vuitton, Prada, and Tiffany's. A few different times, Mike had bought me earrings at Tiffany's, my favorite jewelry store. Although he knew I appreciated fine jewelry, the most meaningful gift he ever bought me was *The Dr. Charles Stanley Life Principles Bible*.

One afternoon after I had finished having my taxes done, Mike suggested, "Let's go to the mall." He introduced me to an acquaintance, Armando, a makeup artist at one of the major department stores. Mike wanted me to feel pampered by having a makeover. I agreed that it would be fun. While Armando used his palette of makeup on me, Mike disappeared. I didn't blame him for his disappearance, because my makeover took a while.

While Mike drifted through the mall, Armando shared with me that Mike had been his personal trainer at the gym years before I had met him. Mike never worked a day while I was with him. He lived off of his inheritance from his father. Armando also shared with me that although it was a gym atmosphere with macho guys everywhere, Mike had treated him with kindness and dignity after learning that Armando was homosexual. He spoke and thought very highly of Mike. A half hour later, Mike still hadn't returned. I wondered where he had disappeared to, yet I was used to his impulsive disappearing acts from shopping with him in the past.

For example, once when we shopped at the grocery store, Mike suddenly disappeared. I searched every aisle, to no avail. I then decided to search the parking lot for him. As I exited the main door, lo and behold, there stood Mike, collecting donations for a local veterans' organization. He wanted to put his time to good use while he waited for me to shop and solicited donations from patrons who entered the store. While I had stressed out searching every inch of the store for him, Mike had had a grand old time laughing with the veterans. How could I get mad at him when he spontaneously helped raise money for a great cause?

After my makeover was finished, Mike appeared. "Wow! Armando did a fantastic job," he said. "You look beautiful. You are the most beautiful woman here at the mall." To my surprise, Mike then handed me a gift with gold wrapping paper and a gold bow. I quickly ripped the wrapping paper off the box. I couldn't wait to see what was inside. Mike had bought me a beautiful diamond necklace while I was having my makeover. The necklace had "two hearts as one." The center heart had diamonds. A few girls who worked with Armando came over to admire it.

One girl told me, "It's exquisite. He has nice taste." Mike made me feel incredibly special and loved that day. He lined up everything, from the makeover to the diamond necklace.

Mike also returned to his passion for cooking. He was a gourmet cook, and I loved anything he made for me. Well, there was one exception. I didn't like his scrambled eggs. I need my scrambled eggs large and fluffy. His were tasty, but not fluffy. Because of my lack of interest in cooking, I always greatly appreciated any meal he cooked. The kitchen was his domain. It was best that I stayed out of the kitchen to give him the space he needed.

Mike was aware that I preferred to eat healthy. I had never been with a man who cared about what I ate. He made sure that I was well fed. He was highly perceptive and immediately knew when I needed to eat. He would look at me and say, "You need something to eat. You're much better after you've eaten." I'm lucky that I have an unusually high metabolism and can eat whatever I want without gaining weight. The downside is that I have to eat every three hours or my thinking becomes foggy and I'm unable to focus clearly. He was never concerned about eating for himself; he had a poor appetite from the alcohol. He placed my needs above his own.

Mike was in tune with my body's needs for food and sleep. He was not only perceptive regarding my needs, but understood me on a deep level. I loved the fact that there was actually somebody in the world who cared about every little detail of my life. I had always desired a deep intimacy and connection with a man. I had finally found that love with Mike. He always wanted me to have the best: the best dinners, cars, jewelry, you name it. He whipped up whatever was in the kitchen, creating delicious meals.

Although Mike continued to create a better life for us, it was far from picture-perfect. He continued with his drinking, but I asked myself, *Can his body be strong enough to handle all this alcohol?* I noticed that as he wore Peter's clothing and watch, he slowly started to take on a bit of Peter's demeanor. It was subtle, but it was there. Also, Mike called and connected with Peter's old girlfriends on the phone. At first it didn't bother me, but as time went by, I questioned why he had drifted onto this path.

I surmised that he found comfort from Peter's friends. Perhaps in some strange way, his brother's friends and clothes helped him feel closer to him. Although we created incredibly special memories there, I concluded that living in Peter's house was a hindrance to Mike's healing from his brother's death. There were too many reminders of his brother that pro-hibited Mike from moving forward. Our dream to start the Christian nonprofit for youth was obviously on hold, as Mike needed to heal from his brother's death and alcohol addiction. I was eager to keep the dream alive in him while we dealt with the issues at hand.

I also noticed that he seemed angrier when he was drinking in the house than when out in the world. I had an acute awareness of the contrast. At times, Mike was difficult or angry in our home, but he seemed dif-ferent—more loving—once we stepped out of the house. Even though he drank vodka before we left the house, I noticed his demeanor changed radically once we were out of the house and running our daily errands.

I also saw in Mike that he loved to encourage others, especially younger people in their twenties. When we bought groceries, he loved to make the clerk smile. Once we were in a restaurant and he asked for the manager to come over. He uplifted one of the employees to the manager's attention because we had received great service that evening. He loved being around people, and I saw his gifts shine through dining experiences and daily errands.

One night after I came home from work, Mike bought me a sandwich at a local sandwich shop. He then asked the young guy behind the counter who had made my sandwich for his name. The next day, Mike called the corporate office of this local restaurant and said, "Steve was outstanding. He went above and beyond, and he should receive a raise." Most follow-up calls from customers in restaurants are complaints, but Mike went out of his way to help build up this young man's confidence. Mike had acted in a biblical way: the Bible says that we are to use our words to encourage and build others up. We are not to criticize and tear down others with our words.

Mike used to say, "I haven't done my job today unless I made one person smile."

I never met a man in all my life whose heart was as pure as Mike's. I loved his heart. That's what I loved most about him. God gave Mike an extraordinary heart. Through his daily actions and the genuine way in which he connected with others, Mike's essence at his core was pure and loving.

# 13

## the Summer from Hell

**July 2013**

S pring flowed into summer rather quickly. As weeks went by, the love I knew and witnessed in Mike was slowly overshadowed by the destructive effects of his intense alcohol consumption. The summer from hell (as I called it) tested every ounce of faith in me. Although I did not attend church at the time, my personal relationship with God through Christ deepened daily. God gave me supernatural strength during that most difficult time. I was torn between the harsh reality of keeping Mike alive and keeping our relationship afloat.

That summer I felt like I was being tossed to and fro by ocean waves as I tried to keep my head above water.

Mike hit a pivotal point that summer with a new state of mental and physical deterioration. His increased alcohol abuse along with having virtually no food for seven months completely altered his being. He switched gears for the worse, because there were no more intercessory periods of jail to keep him sober.

His mental processing combined confusion and aggression at that point. Mike was the strongest person I had ever known, but his alcohol abuse finally caught up to his mind and body. Time became a major factor in the fight for his life; it was a race against time.

However, there was also another fight for his life that became apparent. I entered into a spiritual battle with the Enemy over Mike's life. When I refer to "the Enemy," I am referring to Satan, who the Bible makes clear is out to destroy, to steal, and to kill us. "Be sober, be vigilant; because your adversary the devil walks about like a roaring lion, seeking whom he may devour" (1 Peter 5:8).

The Enemy does not want us to grow close to God. The Bible clearly says that the Enemy has no authority over Christians. I had no fear of the Enemy because of what Christ accomplished for us. Christ victoriously defeated the Enemy at the cross through His resurrection. God had used my past pain and disappointments to strengthen me and equip and prepare me for the battle I was to face.

Mike's drinking switched from beer after his father's death to vodka straight up in a plastic cup after Peter's suicide. Additionally, his anger, fueled by the alcohol, escalated to an all-time high that summer. The Enemy had a stranglehold on Mike. He had anger in his eyes. I found it heart wrenching to witness his countenance. I missed his warm, loving brown eyes that had penetrated me deeply in the past. I felt deep in my gut, *Get ready: you're going into battle.* The fight was on.

I had always fought the good fight for what I believed in. It's part of my nature. I loved Mike with all of my heart, and he was worth fighting for. I had friends who told me to walk away from him, but love and loyalty kept me by Mike's side. According to the Alcoholics Anonymous philosophy, one is to leave the alcoholic alone. I felt that because Mike's brother had committed suicide seven months earlier, I didn't have the heart to leave him alone. Nor could I stand the thought of being away from him for very long. We were inseparable.

Colleen (Peter's girlfriend at the time of his suicide) stayed in touch with Mike and me by phone throughout the seven months after Peter's death. Other than Colleen, none of my friends or family members truly knew what I was experiencing daily with Mike's newly demented frame of mind during that particular summer.

Mike's reality slowly surrendered to delusion and paranoia, forms of disordered thinking. His perception, which had been razor sharp and keen in the past, vanished. Because of his paranoia, he thought I was out to steal from him, even though my actions proved otherwise. For example, one night as I was putting the laundry away, I found Peter's college football ring and an Italian watch hidden in the sock drawer. Another day as I helped Mike close Peter's estate, I found a hundred dollars in cash hidden in an envelope in Peter's filing cabinet.

I had turned over to Mike all of Peter's valuables that I had unexpectedly found. Hypothetically, I could have easily taken Peter's hidden valuables, but I didn't care about any of Peter's belongings, and that would have been stealing. I cared about helping Mike to the best of my ability. Peter's estate was complicated, with ongoing mail from banks and credit card companies to whom he owed money, because he had filed for bankruptcy before his suicide.

Not only did I try to help Mike to the best of my ability, but I tried to rebuild trust with him. I knew that he had difficulty trusting people in general because of his background. I was also aware that I had disappointed him by withdrawing money while he was in prison, even though he had promised that money to me. Mike had already forgiven me for my mistake as I had paid him back. No matter what good deeds I did to rebuild trust with Mike, he suffered from his demons of paranoia and delusion.

Because Mike started drinking vodka shortly after awakening, he was somewhat clear minded in the mornings. Sometimes he drank the vodka with juice, but mostly he drank it straight out of a cup, not even with ice. By the time eight o'clock at night rolled around, he had become unbearable.

I struggled constantly to slow the pace of his alcohol consumption. At first, I tried to control it by hiding his vodka bottles. "What did you do with my bottle, Karen?" Mike asked as he fumed with anger.

"I don't remember where I put it, Mike," I answered dishonestly. I knew it was hidden under my bed. Sometimes I hid it in the hall closet. I chose places where he would never find his bottle.

I then used a strategy that was more subtle. I decided to empty some of the vodka out of the bottle while Mike slept and then partially filled it with water. Because vodka is clear, he wouldn't visibly notice the difference. My strategy worked in the beginning, but he eventually caught on to the diluting because of the lack of taste. In my moments of anger, I threw out the vodka bottles, but he would call taxis to pick him up to buy more. I tried desperately to keep him sober, but my tactics eventually failed. I calculated that he spent nine hundred to a thousand dollars a month on alcohol alone.

After months of engaging in cyclical arguments with him, I finally learned to leave the room and go into another room. It wasn't out of fear that I walked away. I finally smartened up by doing it God's way. This was God's battle.

Mike wanted someone to argue with in his drunken state. I decided I wouldn't give him the time of day when he acted in that manner. A few times when I locked the bedroom door to keep him out, he yelled from the hallway, "Stay in there. Go hide like a little rat." He once placed cheese on the floor outside my door and said in his demented frame of mind, "Here, rat, I left you some cheese to eat."

The food situation became bizarre during that summer. Mike threw out my breakfast cereal, oatmeal, almond milk, yogurts, fruit—virtually anything I ate for breakfast. I strategically hid nonrefrigerated food in my bedroom closet and in a smaller mini-fridge under the bar. He eventually found where I hid my food, and I had to find new places to hide it. When I came home at night after work, the food had been thrown out. I became angry about his juvenile behavior and the fact that he wasted money by throwing out food. Additionally, he kept me from eating breakfast by throwing out my breakfast food. I was already under-weight and too thin from the stress of our arguments that summer. These sick acts were alarming signs of his mental deterioration.

This sick behavior came from a man who a couple of months earlier had loved to cook for me. I was torn between my love for Mike and the need to get away from his destructiveness. However, even as I gave prayerful consideration to leaving that unhealthy envi-ronment, I knew Mike would never physically harm me. He wasn't that type of man. He abhorred the idea of a man hurting a woman. It disgusted him. Additionally, I had no fear of him, for I knew who he was at his core.

Soon, I noticed that several toiletries from my bath-room were gone. My aloe vera gel, body lotions, and shampoo had been thrown out. I rushed to the garbage bags in the hot, humid garage to search for them. To my surprise, I found a black pinstriped pencil skirt that Mike had bought for me in the bottom of a garbage bag. I had no clue that any clothes had been thrown out, as I didn't wear formal clothing often.

Luckily, I remembered that there were keys in the kitchen drawer, one of which locked the closet door in my bedroom. I quickly gathered the majority of my belongings and valuables such as my jewelry box and placed them in the locked closet. I thought my belong-ings were now safe and protected.

The next day when I was leaving the house to do an errand, I saw that the front two tires of the car were dangerously low. As I stooped down, I observed that the caps were missing from them. The car had been parked in the garage overnight. I knew that the bizarre act had been done by Mike.

I anxiously drove to the closest gas station, pretty shaken up. I frantically asked a stranger for help in putting air in the tires. I had no idea how many pounds of pressure were supposed to go into them. I was grateful that a stranger took time to help me. I felt beyond drained at that point. That day pushed me to the edge. I felt like I had hit rock bottom. I would no longer allow this hardship. I knew I had to leave.

The day felt surreal. I felt like I couldn't go on anymore. I couldn't deal with the emotional pain, and became emotionally numb. I couldn't even emote tears of sadness. I wanted desperately to feel normal, like my old self again. I thought to myself, *Please, somebody help me.* At that moment, I felt a spiritual prompting that I didn't need an actual person to help me. If I pressed into God more deeply, He would lighten my yoke. Although I always had God's promise of His presence, I struggled back and forth once again, trying to handle a situation on my own. I wanted to be in control instead of letting God fight the battle for me.

For example, several nights later, I overheard Mike call an escort service. I wavered back into my control mode. I grabbed the phone out of his hand and disconnected the call. He became angry with me for taking his phone and said in his drunken stupor, "Well, you never have sex with me anymore, so I have to take care of my needs."

I responded in a logical manner (forgetting for a moment that Mike had become delusional) and said, "Why would you expect me to be physically intimate with you? You've blatantly disrespected me with your out-of-control, demented behavior."

I stormed out of the bedroom. Next, I proceeded to tear out the pages listing escort services from several phone books in an attempt to stop him from making those kinds of calls. Additionally, I waited until he fell asleep to delete the numbers of the services from his cell phone. I felt I needed to protect us and our home from the filth he brought into our lives. God revealed truth to me with what followed.

One night I drove home around ten o'clock after getting off work. As always, I entered through the guarded gate into where we lived in Boca Pointe. That night was particularly unbelievable. I pulled up behind an older station wagon as I waited for entry through the gate. I rolled down my window as I prepared to say hello to the night guard. I overheard the woman in the station wagon in front of my car say to the gate guard, "Hi, I'm a friend of Mike P. I'm here to see him."

I couldn't believe what I had heard, as well as the timing. With my car running and my blood raging, I got out of my car and walked straight to her window. In front of the gate guard, I announced to the unknown woman, "I'm Mike's fiancée. Can I help you with any-thing?" I knew that she was an escort. The gate guard had already called Mike, who was on his way to the gate to let her in, because he obviously hadn't put her name on the gate guard's entry list.

She looked quite embarrassed as her voice quiv-ered, "I'm sorry, ma'am. I don't mean to cause any trouble." She immediately turned her car around and left quickly before Mike arrived.

It appeared I had caught Mike red-handed. Once in the house, my anger exploded. I yelled, "Mike, you are out of control and need help. How could you do that to us? You've been the most loyal man I've known. Secondly, who takes an escort to a home in this type of neighborhood in Boca Raton? She could have had a pimp in the car with her. They could have stolen from our home and killed you, Mike." At that point, I knew a dangerous combination was driving Mike's decisions. The Enemy's evil pervaded our lives, combined with Mike's mental decline.

Mike replied, "I walked down to the gate to tell her to go home." He continued, "I couldn't go through with it. I kept thinking of you, and I couldn't do it. That is the truth, Karen."

"Yeah, right, Mike," I retorted. "You expect me to believe that? I got out of my car to introduce myself to the woman. She immediately turned her car around and left in embarrassment. I don't believe you." Deep down I truly wanted to believe him, but I wouldn't give him the satisfaction in that moment, because I was hurt and angry.

When the escort idea failed, Mike took taxis to strip clubs. He had never frequented strip clubs while living with me. He was out of control and mentally deranged, and the Enemy was out to destroy our relationship. The Enemy had a stranglehold on Mike and wanted me out of the picture. I was the obstacle to be removed. Except for God, I was the only one who fought to keep Mike alive. It was out of my love and loyalty for Mike that I stayed that summer. I feared that if I left him alone, it would be only a matter of time before destruction and thus death would prevail. In essence, I feared that if I left Mike, he would die.

Mike couldn't grasp that I loved him to the point that I fought to keep him alive. Instead, he believed and bought into the Enemy's lie in regard to my purpose for being with him. Mike's delusional mind believed that I was his enemy. The Enemy uses deception and division to destroy us. Jesus called him a murderer and the father of lies in John 8:44. The Enemy instigates pain, sorrow, addiction, and death everywhere. When the Enemy speaks through others, he accuses and deceives. He condemns, antagonizes, and confuses us to fill us with doubt and despair.

One evening as I read the Bible, Mike approached me and said, "You don't know anything about the Bible." I felt an evil spirit's presence when he spoke those words.

"Leave me alone. I wasn't bothering you. I was reading quietly in my room. Now again, leave," I told him emphatically. Of course, he wouldn't leave.

The evil spirit used Mike as a provocateur to turn the heat up a notch. "You don't really know God," he said.

In that moment, I remembered that one should never try to reason with an evil spirit, but should rebuke it in the name of Jesus. I retorted, "Get behind me, Satan" referring to the verse in Matthew 16:23.

I stood in armor with the Bible as my shield as I read out loud. "No weapon formed against me can prosper," I declared.

My stomach turned with sickness, because I knew an evil spirit had attacked me through Mike's words. As angry as I became with Mike, I tried to remain calm.

I remembered an earlier conversation with Miriam about his provoking comments. "Those comments are evil spirits attacking you through Mike," she once shared with me when she came to clean the house.

God was my protector, my fortress, and my refuge in that darkness. **God's promise of protection** was fulfilled in my life. Oddly, with all the distress I suffered, I slept peacefully every night. "He who dwells in the secret place of the Most High shall abide under the shadow of the Almighty. I will say of the Lord, 'He is my refuge and my fortress; My God, in Him I will trust'" (Psalm 91:1–2).

I felt I had no friend or family member to turn to because of the shame I thought it would bring. Although evil escalated in our home, I learned to trust God, whom I turned to morning, day, and night. God supplied me with supernatural strength. Most women probably would not have been able to handle the intensity that I endured, but God had prepared me. I was like steel inside. I was fearless. It's not to say that the situation didn't wear me down at times. It did, but I knew what my limitations were.

Additionally, the Mike whom I had loved when he was sober and of sound mind would never have behaved that way or spoken those deplorable, vile words. However, the times had changed, and Mike's destructiveness was in full throttle. Watching the man I loved slowly destroy himself left me emotionally devastated beyond words. It broke my heart, because I loved Mike with all of my being.

Although I had no control over his evil comments, I could remove myself from his presence. I lived on my side of the house and he lived on his side. Luckily, our bedrooms were on opposite sides of the house. In an attempt to test Mike's faith, I said, "Mike, let's read the Bible together like we used to do in the past." But he wanted nothing to do with the Bible.

I thought to myself, *What happened to the old Mike who loved staying up late talking with me about the Bible and our faith when we first met? Where did he go?*

I want to be clear in saying that I do not believe Mike was "possessed" by the Enemy. I believe that he was "oppressed" by the Enemy, with demonic spirits surrounding him. Demonic spirits can enter through gateways of both alcoholism and anger. He did not need a formal exorcism by a priest. He needed to be set free once again from the bondage of alcoholism. God had graciously set him free through the miracle with Miriam. Tragically, he had chosen to go back to the path of alcoholism and destruction.

That summer, I suffered tremendous verbal and psychological abuse in a home pervaded by evil. Although I tried to ignore Mike's provoking insults by leaving the room, I slipped at times and reverted to verbal attacks in retaliation. My natural inclination was to defend myself. Because of my temperament, when Mike provoked me, it was easier for me to fight back than to allow my spiritual side to prevail.

I once took a Ping golf club and accidentally shattered the glass desk in the office into thousands of pieces. We had argued in the dark office and I had held the golf club vertically over my head, shouting angrily, "I can't take this anymore. You need to stop now." Next, glass shattered in all directions. Luckily, neither one of us was hurt, but I know that once I am provoked to that level, I have a temper. Mike provoked my anger in ways that were out of character for me.

The Enemy surely loved seeing Mike and I destroy each other as we tore at each other's throats with unkind sentiments. However, the Enemy may have won the battle, but the war was not over. Somewhere in that ugliness, when I was alone, I dropped to my knees and asked God to help me. Somehow, some way, God revealed to me that there was victory in Christ if I followed God's ways and not my fleshly ways of trying to regain leverage.

After a traumatic summer of Mike's rage from alcoholism, I eventually learned to slowly surrender the turmoil to God. As much as I tried to bring Mike to the light, I ultimately learned that this was God's battle with Mike, not mine. It was best if I removed myself. I also realized that I enabled Mike's drinking by assuming all responsibility for the household. God grew me in profound ways.

Although God prepared me with the warning of the battle, scripture had taught me to press into God. I wavered back and forth, trying to win the battle "my way." However, I eventually learned that summer that I couldn't fight any spiritual battle on my own. When I prayed for God's wisdom and discernment over the matter, I depended on God's power. The concept of asking God for help was initially hard for me because of my independent nature, which tried to fix all problems on my own. However, I relied on my past experiences of God's faithfulness when He victoriously brought me through the dark trials of abandonment when I first moved to Florida.

One of my favorite scriptures, "I can do all things through Christ who strengthens me," Philippians 4:13, sustained me during the darkness and hardship of that summer. **God's promise of strength** infused me with new strength and empowerment. God's love changed me forevermore during that critical time of my life. I don't know how I would have survived without God's grace and unconditional love.

Meanwhile, as I prepared to transition out of our home to keep my sanity, God taught me to show kindness to Mike even while Mike devalued me. Jesus taught us to love our enemy. When Mike hurled insults at me, I was led to not only pray for him, but extend kindness and love to him—not an easy task by any means. However, I continually asked God to help me, and with practice it became easier to respond to Mike's angry behavior through God's way.

We are to be merciful with the unjust, just as God our Father has been merciful to us. By learning the valuable lesson of handling Mike through God's ways and not my fleshly ways of responding to his attacks, my faith grew by leaps and bounds. If my faith was truly being tested during that trial period, I believe I grew exponentially that summer.

I victoriously learned that when evil strikes, I am to respond with love.

God wants us to show value to those who devalue us. I trust that my worthiness comes from God and not from any person. I learned to trust God for my way out of the darkness. The Bible says that we are to pray for those who mistreat us.

"But I say to you who hear: Love your enemies, do good to those who hate you. Bless those who curse you, and pray for those who spitefully use you" (Luke 6:27–28).

# 14

## Two Doors Open Simultaneously

**August 2013**

*After battling evil spirits, what is there to be afraid of?* I had faced evil, demonic spirits and through Christ was victorious. God carried me in the palm of His hand. No one can snatch us from the power of God's hand. Letting go of control and turning my circumstances over to God was the key. I was trying to be in control of the battle, but it was never my battle to begin with. It was God's battle.

Through the process, God toughened me with an inner strength and the knowledge that no situation or person could ever intimidate me into leaving my home. I had no reason to fear the Enemy because of my faith in God's protection over me.

Later, in retrospect, I understood that I was meant to learn a lesson about conflict. It would have been easier to leave immediately after Mike's bizarre and hurtful acts that summer. However, I had to learn invaluable lessons by not running but standing my ground. I learned that we gain strength and power from knowing God's ways through scripture and prayer. God's word was an immovable anchor during the uncertainty of the circumstances I faced.

And last but not least, I knew that forevermore, whatever God allowed, no matter how horrendous the situation, He could turn it around for our good.

"And we know that all things work together for good to those who love God, to those who are the called according to His purpose" (Romans 8:28).

God doesn't desire for His children to live in ongoing abusive situations. God was about to open a new door for me.

I began to search the classifieds online for a new home and started to make plans for my exit strategy. My weary soul had taken all that I could take. In my efforts to love Mike to the best of my ability, I knew deep down I had to love myself by leaving that unhealthy environment.

Colleen, Peter's former girlfriend, and her roommate Kim were instrumental in finding me a new home. Because of my newly leased car and my expenses being greater than my income, I wasn't sure how it would all pan out with renting a new home. I didn't want to struggle financially after the weariness I had experienced with Mike. Sure enough, God provided a way out of what seemed impossible.

After all the emotional pain I had endured, God provided me with a beautiful, five-bedroom waterfront home to live in, manage, and assist with while the owner, who lived in New York, visited one weekend out of the month. My new job was to care for the home, and in exchange I didn't have to pay rent. It was a barter situation. It was a godsend. After the nightmare of the summer I had endured, I was grateful to Colleen and Kim, who found this home through an online search. Colleen knew some of what I had experienced with Mike's deteriorating mental state, not only from my conversations with her, but from receiving a disturbing call from him.

One night, Mike, in his drunkenness, called Colleen. After he didn't reach her, he left a message in her voice mail. He asked, "Colleen, why did you have to do it? Why did you have to kill my brother? Couldn't the two of you have worked things out?"

Although Mike grieved deeply, his mental processing was skewed. He had already received the autopsy report from the detective saying that Peter's death was indeed a suicide.

"Karen, he's sick," Colleen said. "He's mentally deranged to be leaving that kind of message. This is very upsetting to me. I can't deal with him anymore. I'm changing my number." She changed it immediately.

She had witnessed a mere fraction of the deterioration that I had experienced with Mike. She too was grieving in a deep place of pain over Peter's death. She didn't need the aggravation Mike had caused her.

Additionally, she became concerned about me. One night before I had moved out of the house, Colleen and I conversed on the phone. I was sitting on the platform bed when Mike barged into my bedroom. He demanded, "Who are you speaking to on the phone?"

"Mike, please leave me alone. I'm on the phone. I'll be out in the living room shortly," I said. He had rudely interrupted my phone call.

Colleen asked me, "Karen, are you okay? I don't like how he's talking to you. I'm concerned about your safety."

"I'm fine, Colleen," I assured her. "I've been through worse. I want to thank you and Kim for finding this new home for me. I have to wait just a few more weeks before I can move in." Her support meant a great deal to me. She and Kim had taken time out of their busy schedules in New Jersey to find me a safe home in Florida.

We got off the phone. An hour later, the doorbell rang. I thought to myself, *Who could be ringing our doorbell this late at night?* It was ten o'clock at night. I answered the door and was surprised to find two police officers standing there.

"Good evening, ma'am. We received a phone call from a Colleen in New Jersey who was concerned about your safety," one of the officers informed me.

I invited them inside to assure them that I was not in any imminent danger. The one officer took Mike outside to question him on the front lawn while the other officer questioned me in the living room. The officer said, "If your fiancé made any threats to your well-being, you have the right to have him arrested."

"That won't be necessary," I told the officer. "He's been drinking and was in one of his argumentative moods. I wouldn't be living here if I didn't feel safe."

The officer concluded his visit and headed toward the foyer to leave. He said, "We will sit outside your home for a little while, but we cannot stay here all night."

I thanked the officer for his time and assured him that I slept on my side of the house and Mike stayed on his side of the house. Mike was certainly surprised to see the police at our door, especially since he had finished with his legal entanglements. He definitely did not want any more trouble. However, he was aware that I was not the one who made the call to the police, but that the call had come from a "concerned friend."

Although I was extremely grateful about moving into a new home within a few weeks, my interview before I received the job came with an unexpected challenge. As I left to go to the interview to manage the waterfront property, Mike followed me out the door and into the passenger seat of our car.

I explained to Mike, "I will be back in an hour. I have an interview for a new job." Then I said firmly, "Mike, you need to get out of the car now, because I have an interview. I don't want to be late." He wouldn't budge from the passenger seat of the car. He had been drinking, was irrational, and caused unnecessary tension. I didn't have time for an argument or I would have been late to the interview.

"Fine, I will drop you off at the convenience store and you can walk or take a taxi back, okay?" I said anxiously with no time to debate. He agreed. As soon as I pulled in to the closest store, Mike dropped his end of the bargain. He refused to get out of the car. Panic struck me. *What am I to do? He can't come with me to this interview. This is my worst nightmare,* I thought to myself as my heart raced. He must have sensed that I desired to move out of our home.

"Mike, get out of the car now. You're not coming with me to this interview. You're not going to screw up this interview. Why can't you keep your end of the deal? I said I'd give you a ride. I'll be home in about an hour." I was fuming.

"No, I'm going with you," he said stubbornly.

I continued driving to my appointment. I was less than five minutes away from where the interview was to take place when Mike shouted, "Let me out here at the convenience store on the left." I thanked God for the intervention.

"Mike, stay put and I'll pick you up on my way back from the interview." I sighed with relief. My nerves were shot as I tried to recompose myself. I walked into the interview confidently with my head up and shoulders back as if nothing had happened. By the grace of God I landed the job.

After the interview about the waterfront property, I drove back to pick up Mike at the convenience store. He had vanished and was nowhere to be found. The store clerk informed me that Mike had asked him to call for a taxi to take him home.

I eagerly looked forward to my new home and job as caretaker and personal assistant to the owner, who lived in New York. When the day had arrived for me to move out, I packed my car quickly and quietly like a fire drill. Mike napped that afternoon. I didn't wake him because I didn't want a scene. I didn't tell Mike about my decision to move out. I thought that given his mental state, it was best to tell him afterward. I hated the notion of leaving him all alone. However, I had become too thin, and my voice was hoarse from the stress of our arguments. Tragically, I had seen the man I loved deteriorate mentally and physically before my eyes.

When Mike called me a few days later, he was surprised I had left without telling him. He never asked me to move back in with him. Although I still loved him deeply, I had to remain strong without him. After I moved out, I wasn't heartbroken like I thought I would be. I guess I believed deep down that we would be reunited again someday. I decided to remain friends with him. I had decided that Mike would have to stay sober for at least one year before I would reconsider any type of life with him. Furthermore, my body and soul had become drained from the summer to the point that it was easier for me to stay away from Mike than it had been in the past.

As time went on, I offered to help Mike on a weekly basis with groceries because he didn't have a driver's license or car. I made it clear to him that I would in no way help him buy alcohol. By that point, I hated alcohol, detested it for the destruction that had taken place within Mike and within us.

October 2013

Two months after I settled into my new place, Mike's cousin Melanie expressed to him that she planned to visit him during October. While I visited with Mike one night, he asked me to talk to Melanie on the phone and get the details of her flight. I took her number and called her later when I returned home.

I tried to warn Melanie about Mike's mental deterioration and how sick he had become. I tried my best to prepare her for the reality that lay ahead if she came to visit him.

"Hi, Melanie, I am looking forward to meeting you," I assured her warmly. "Mike has told me that you are the only family he has. I will pick you up at the airport and drive you back to your departing flight as well. I have to be honest with you about Mike's condition. He is not as mentally strong as he used to be. Sadly, he has become mentally paranoid and has not eaten very much food in the last ten months since Peter's suicide. His alcoholism is out of control. I have tried every possible way to get him the help he desperately needs, but he refuses to get help."

I continued, "I know you have many special memories of when Mike would visit you in Texas. He told me he would take you shopping when you were a young girl because he loved to spoil you. I feel you are going to be in for quite a shock at the picture you see when you arrive. I know Mike would love to have the support from a family member, but I don't think it is in your best interest to stay in the house with him. I no longer live with Mike because I had to move out. He's become too unstable."

She didn't hear a word I said. Instead of asking probing questions about Mike's mental condition, she replied, "It will be great. Mike can teach me how to make lasagna. I really miss him."

I knew she was in for a rude awakening and did everything I could to try to deter her from coming. She had never been to the palace in Boca Raton, since she hadn't been as close with Peter as she was with Mike.

I picked up Melanie and her little Chihuahua at the Fort Lauderdale airport and took her to Mike's house after we stopped for some dinner. I knew there was probably little to no food at Mike's house. The next day I took the two of them grocery shopping. Later that night, Mike cooked a great dinner for Melanie and me. Melanie's visit appeared to have no problems until the next day, when I received a phone call from her.

"Hi, Karen, this is Melanie. Mike won't let me into the house. I took my dog for a walk around the block, and he won't let me back into the house," she cried into the phone. I heard the fear in her voice. Luckily, I lived only ten to fifteen minutes away.

"I'll be right over. I'll meet you at the bench across from the security gate where cars enter," I assured her. When I arrived, Melanie seemed emotionally distraught. Although I had kept a key to the house, I knocked at the door to see if Mike would answer. He opened the door for me and let her in as well.

"Mike, what was that about? Why didn't you let Melanie into the house?" I inquired.

He replied, "I want her and her dog completely out of the house. I don't like her attitude." I didn't probe any further. I had no clue about why he had behaved that way other than his usual mental state. Sadly, his paranoia and delusions dictated his decisions in a way that was similar to what I had experienced with him.

I had tried to warn Melanie before her visit. Luckily, she had a friend in Miami who invited her for a visit. I drove her to and from the train station so she could get to Miami and back. Upon leaving for the airport, she needed a little more money for the extra fee for traveling with her dog. Mike helped her with the money, and they said goodbye. I drove Melanie to the airport for her flight back to Austin.

While Melanie stayed with Mike, she sold a few of Peter's sports memorabilia items to help him. When Peter committed suicide three weeks after appearing on television, the producers of the show had offered free grief therapy to the family. I had tried to convince Mike to accept their gracious offer but he declined any help. Melanie, with her computer-savvy research skills, opened a door with the producers and reached them by phone.

The producers at the show were deeply moved by Mike's story and offered to pay for his treatment for addiction at one of the most prestigious clinics in the country. Airfare was not included. Mike would pay for his airfare to the recovery center in Texas, but he initially procrastinated in acting on the incredible opportunity of healing as the power of his addiction fed his drinking.

At first, Mike was somewhat reluctant, but he eventually agreed that the offer was a once-in-a-lifetime opportunity not to be missed. One afternoon while at his home, we sat on the patio furniture on the lanai. He grabbed my hand in excitement and looked straight into my eyes with determination as he said, "Let's do this." I smiled back and without hesitation grabbed my cell phone to make the call to the admissions office at the recovery center. Mike was determined to heal. He accepted their gracious offer to the road of recovery.

God lovingly opened two doors simultaneously. First, I had moved miraculously to a new waterfront home with no monthly rental. Second, Mike was open and willing to travel to the best addiction recovery center in the country, where his treatment would be paid for in full. I thanked God for answering my prayers. I was grateful not only to the producers at the show, but also to Melanie for her help and tenacity. Melanie opened the door as she conveyed to the staff Mike's deteriorating condition. Finally, Mike was able to receive the counseling and treatment he desperately needed. I saw light at the end of the tunnel.

# 15

## the final fight

**December 2013**

Christmas crept up on us rather quickly. From the new home in Deerfield Beach where I had moved, I called the addiction recovery center in Texas. I asked the admissions counselor, "What date are we looking at for admitting Mike into the center?"

The admissions counselor answered, "I'm sorry, but due to the holiday season, there are no beds available at this time."

"What? Oh no, this is not what I was expecting to hear. Is there anything you can do to speed up the process? Mike cannot wait another four weeks, as Christmas is fast approaching. I'm concerned that the holidays will increase his drinking. I saw what happened last Christmas after his brother committed suicide. Please, can you check availability again for me?" I pleaded.

The counselor empathetically replied, "Mike is next on the waiting list. I will call you as soon as a bed becomes available, hopefully within the next few weeks."

My heart sank with sadness over the news. Mike needed to be there before Christmas. Although he was accepted into the recovery program, sadly, time was not on our side. We were hit with an unbelievable obstacle, having to wait two to four weeks until a bed was available. I pushed relentlessly, placing numerous phone calls to the counselor in Texas regarding availability for Mike's admission.

One sunny afternoon, Mike and I shopped as Christmas music filled the air. Under the store's fluorescent lighting, my jaw dropped in shock as I gazed into Mike's eyes and face. His jaundiced eyes were a shade of yellow that I'd never seen before in my life. His belly had bloated to the size of a watermelon because of his liver. He had great difficulty standing in the store for more than five minutes. "Karen, you finish shopping. I'm going to sit on the bench outside of the store," Mike informed me. All those signs of fragility indicated to me that he had lost his normal strength and energy.

As soon as we returned to Mike's home, I called 911 and had a paramedic/ambulance come to the house to take him to the closest hospital. While I waited in the emergency room, the doctor informed me that his liver was failing. The liver is the most resilient organ in the body. A human liver can grow back even after 75 percent of it has been removed. I prayed and claimed victory in faith over Mike's situation. He was immediately admitted to the hospital.

I called Lefty after leaving Mike's hospital room to inform him of Mike's situation. Lefty was Mike's second

"Dad." Mike shared a close bond with Lefty, who had been his father's close friend from the military. When Mike moved to South Korea to be with his father in his twenties, he met Lefty and had remained friends ever since. Lefty was a great support to me in those days. I had never met him, but I'd had phone conversations with him when Mike and I lived together. I knew it gave Mike great comfort to have Lefty in his life after his father passed away.

The doctors were able to stabilize Mike after a month of care in the hospital. I thanked God for answering my prayer. I saw the power of faith at work as God was in control of Mike's situation. He was due to be released several days before Christmas with heart failure and a weak liver.

Before his release, I pleaded desperately with the social worker at the hospital. "I am requesting that Mike not be released from the hospital quite yet." With Christmas only days away, I knew he would fall into the same trap of drinking again. With the diagnosis of heart and liver failure, he couldn't afford to be separated from a doctor's care.

The social worker had no empathy. She explained, "We can no longer keep a patient once the doctor has signed the order for his discharge."

I later learned that the hospital has a responsibility for the patient's safety regarding their discharge. I believed his discharge from the hospital was handled incorrectly.

*Wasn't he placed under psychological evaluation from his primary doctor while in the hospital?* I asked myself. Surely, with Christmas only a week away, they must have known his discharge was unsafe. Perhaps they didn't care.

As Mike's advocate, I strongly attempted to strategically line up his exit from the hospital. My plan was to have him go directly from the hospital in Florida to the recovery clinic for addictions in Texas, with no stops in between. I didn't want him to go back to Peter's house alone, particularly at Christmastime.

After no prior availability, there was finally a space available for Mike at the recovery center that the show had generously agreed to pay for thanks to Melanie's diligence.

However, after we received the green light for Texas, we faced a second obstacle. The counselor informed me on the phone, "I'm sorry to tell you that Mike is now considered a medical liability due to his liver and heart failure. We are unable to admit him because he has no insurance. I'm really sorry about this, Karen. I wish there was more that I could do."

After we had waited weeks for a bed to become available, learning that he was a medical liability was too much to bear. I was devastated. Once again, another attempt at getting Michael the help he desperately needed had fallen through. If his physical condition hadn't failed so rapidly, he would have been admitted to the recovery center. I raced against the clock to keep him alive. The fight for his life was now or never.

Additionally, the plane ticket I had booked a few months earlier to visit my mother in Pennsylvania for Christmas created a major challenge. If Mike was left alone at Christmas, it would be detrimental to his health. I invited him to come home with me to my mother's for the holiday. Mike had become sober after a monthlong stay in the hospital. He declined my invitation. He wished to stay alone in Peter's house in Boca Raton, which was a mistake.

I flew into Philadelphia, and my uncle Bob picked me up at the airport. I gained strength from being with family, experiencing a great visit first with my uncle and my cousins, whom I had not seen in a while. The next day, I took the train from Philadelphia to Lewistown to spend a wonderful Christmas with my mother. It was an unbelievably cold and windy Christmas Eve. My mom and I continued our tradition and attended the beautiful candlelight Christmas Eve service at church. The next morning, I woke up and immediately called Mike. We talked long distance for hours on our cell phones. How my heart ached for him, knowing he was alone on Christmas Day.

## January 2014

I returned to South Florida from my mom's home the day before New Year's Eve. As I predicted, Mike had resumed his heavy drinking while I was at my mother's. Upon returning, I immediately went to see him. As I walked into the house, I saw that the elegant home in Boca Pointe was no longer elegant. The electricity had been shut off. The bathrooms were atrocious from his body slowly breaking down. To say that the house was in terrible disarray would be an understatement. Mike looked horrible. I knew I had to act swiftly.

I called the female detective who had handled Peter's suicide case and explained to her how Mike's drinking had steadily increased over the twelve months since his brother's suicide. I informed her that he had severe mental and physical deterioration from malnourishment and that he had been diagnosed with heart and liver failure. I needed help with an intervention.

"I don't have much time. I need help," I said frantically.

"I will send a police officer out immediately to assess the situation." She suggested that Mike be "Baker Acted" into a hospital. Under Florida's Baker Act, a person can be involuntarily institutionalized if it's determined that he intends to harm himself or others.

She immediately called the police on my behalf, and a few officers arrived at the house. They witnessed Mike's unstable state and the horrible condition of the house. Mike was being pulled under as though he were in quicksand. An officer asked him, "Can you tell me what day of the week it is? Who is the president of our country?"

Mike failed to answer any of the basic questions correctly. Between not answering the questions correctly and the state the house was in, it was a no-brainer that Mike could no longer remain in the house. He could no longer take care of himself. The ugly disease of alcoholism had manifested itself into full-blown self-destruction.

Mike was "Baker Acted" to a new hospital, where a security guard sat outside his room twenty-four hours a day. Mike couldn't leave the hospital room even if he tried. Only a doctor could determine when to lift the Baker Act that had been placed upon him. I visited with him every day that I could. I balanced my job with the responsibilities of caring for my new home while being by Mike's side on my days off. I prayed that he would heal and that we would never have to go through any more insanity with his alcoholism.

After Mike became somewhat stabilized, the doctor lifted the Baker Act after a month. The social worker at the hospital fervently tried to arrange for Mike to be transferred to a psychiatric ward at a new hospital in Delray Beach, because the present hospital had no mental health center. After a couple of failed attempts at being transferred to the mental health center for psychiatric evaluation, he was admitted to a new hospital. He had failed to be admitted to the mental health center because he couldn't use the restroom on his own, which was a requirement. His body could no longer function without a catheter.

Several times I brought Mike a fruit salad and a spinach salad when I visited him, because I knew the hospital food wasn't the most nutritious, although it sustained him.

During one particular visit in the new hospital, Mike wavered in and out of a mental state of confusion. He gazed into my eyes as I sat in the chair next to his bed.

"Do I have to be in court today?" he asked me.

I replied, "No, my love, that's all over. You will never have to go to court again." I saw the confusion and fear in his eyes. The bad memories of jail and the pressures of court had sunk deeply into Mike's psyche, where he wavered in and out of delusions.

During his stay in the new hospital, we were informed that Mike was eligible for hospice. That particular hospital had a hospice wing. Mike and I first discussed the matter privately. I guided him to the best of my ability. I felt that he would be under the care he needed, as he could no longer care for himself. My heart sank over the harsh reality that his time left on earth was limited. I feared for his survival as I tried to fight back tears. We then spoke to the hospice counselor and let her know Mike had decided to be transferred to hospice.

After Mike was transferred to hospice, I visited with him the day after his first night's stay. I already noticed significant changes in his demeanor. He appeared extremely tired and withdrawn. I questioned the nurse on duty about his noticeably different behavior. Mike appeared indifferent about his situation. The nurse informed me that he purposely wouldn't allow himself to sleep at night and had been restless throughout the whole night. I learned during my visit that his last day in the hospital before being transferred to the hospice wing had been a pivotal turning point.

His doctor had said to Mike point-blank, "You are going to die." I was furious with the doctor when I heard that. I don't know in what tone or context that statement had been made, but Mike was not the same. He appeared devastated and withdrawn. I intuitively believed that those powerful words from the doctor had totally diminished Mike's hope of recovery. I also believed that Mike became paralyzed with fear that if he fell asleep, he would not wake up. Thus, he refused to sleep.

I cannot imagine what he must have felt in his final days. His final words to others were always of hope and courage. He possessed more strength than any other man I'd known. For the six weeks that Mike had been sober in the hospital before being transferred to hospice, he had returned to his dream of the two of us marrying and spending the rest of our lives together. He frequently shared this hope with his nurses, as well as the chaplain who visited with him. He told the doctor and nurses that I was his fiancée and that I was to be informed at all times of his medical condition. Although the current laws allow only immediate family to learn of the patient's medical condition, the hospital staff knew that I was his only visitor, that I was Mike's caretaker.

Mike's wishes had placed me in an awkward position. He asked me not to contact any of his family members regarding his condition in hospice. In the end, I was all that he had. Fortunately, the medical staff was aware and bent the rules to inform me at all times.

I visited with Mike the day before Valentine's Day. As I drove to hospice, I reminisced about how he and I had decided to live together on Valentine's Day exactly three years earlier. Ironically, our love had started on Valentine's Day weekend. I walked into his hospice room with his favorite white-chocolate-covered pretzels, red roses, and a card that expressed my deep love for him. He was quite happy about the heart-shaped chocolate-covered pretzels and gobbled them up quickly.

It was unbelievable that after everything we had been through in the previous fourteen months, including his brother's suicide and our no longer living together because of his alcoholism, we had somehow miraculously found our way back to love. We had almost destroyed the love that God gave to us as a gift. How symbolic that the day before Valentine's Day we found ourselves utterly and completely loving each other unconditionally.

The following day, on Valentine's Day, I made several attempts to call Mike. He never picked up the hospice phone next to his bed, which was unusual. I then called the nurse with my concern. The nurse explained, "I'm sorry to tell you that Mike has lost his ability to speak." I felt overly confused and intensely upset by the gripping news.

"What do you mean he cannot speak?" I asked the nurse firmly, and then continued, "I just spoke with him yesterday. He had an enjoyable visit from the chaplain as well."

I rushed over to the hospice wing in the hospital after work at midnight to be with Mike. I wanted him to recover. I felt angry that I could not do more to help him. There was nothing I could do except draw near to God and ask for strength in prayer. God's strength lifted me in that confusing web of a dark night.

The next morning, I awoke to a call from his doctor in hospice, who informed me that Mike had twenty-four to forty-eight hours to live. It was a Sunday morning. I prayed, got dressed, and immediately went to be with him. I knew the end was near.

I arrived at Mike's sunny room in hospice, which looked more like a hotel room than a room in a hospital. The nurses made Mike as comfortable as possible. One of them said, "Mike can hear everything you say; he just cannot speak. His voice is paralyzed."

I sat next to where Mike lay on his bed and held his hand. Directly next to his bed was a CD player with a few CDs. I decided to play some soothing music for us and fill the room with it. I tried to make Mike as comfortable as possible. I prepared the room to the best of my ability by providing him with an atmosphere of peace and love.

I then lay my body next to his in the hospice bed, holding him carefully so that I didn't place too much of my body weight on him. I knew his body was fragile. I expressed my love to Mike repeatedly. "I love you more than you know." I then shared with him, "God loves you so much." I desired that his final hours on earth be filled with love poured into his heart.

I then said, "I like this music, Mike. I hope you are enjoying the music from the CD as much as I am." I gazed into his loving, brown eyes and discovered that he could indeed respond to me through his eyes.

When he liked what I said, he raised his eyebrows up and down. Although he could not speak, we had found a way to communicate. He expressed himself through his eyes. He had lost not only the ability to speak, but the ability to move his body. No longer could he move his arms to hold me in that special way that he had, so I held him. Through my body, I poured every ounce of love that I possessed into him. I thanked God that our final day together was filled with love and peace. God's presence and peace filled the sunny hospice room. It didn't matter that we couldn't converse, because those final hours were incredibly special.

Later, in the early evening, I needed something light to eat. I told Mike, "I'm going to this Jewish deli around the corner from the hospital to get some matzo ball soup. I'll be back in fifteen minutes or so." I repeated myself at least two or three times so that he would know for certain that I was returning. It was important to me that Mike understood that I would be right back.

Upon returning to the hospital, I quickly called my father from my car in the parking lot to inform him of Mike's condition. "Hi, Dad. I'm at the hospital with Mike. His doctor told me that he only has twenty-four to forty-eight hours to live. This is the hardest thing I've ever gone through in my adult life. I love him very much."

My dad blurted, "Well, Mike did this to himself." Perhaps my father felt that I shouldn't feel any guilt, but his cold, critical remark shocked me in my time of need.

It was understood that Mike's depression and emotional pain had led to his drinking, which led to his liver disease. It didn't help matters in that critical time as I reached out to my father for love and support.

Disappointed with my father's call, I proceeded toward the hospice wing. I noticed that I had missed a call from an "unknown" number while I was talking with my dad. My first thought was that the call had come from the hospice nurse. My heart raced in panic as I rushed upstairs to Mike's room and walked in briskly. Mike's face was frozen, with no sound of the heavy breathing I had heard all afternoon. I ran to get the hospice nurse. "Something is terribly wrong with Mike," I told her. She followed me into the room.

I knew in my heart that Mike had left to be with the Lord. I needed her to confirm what I knew to be true. The nurse said, "It is quite common for those who are dying to wait for their loved ones to leave the room before they pass." God, in His perfect timing, had waited until I left to get some soup. I also believed that the "unknown" phone call had come from Mike at the time that he had passed.

The nurse warmly offered, "You can stay with Mike or you can wait in the hospice family room, wherever you are most comfortable." There was no way I could sit with his corpse. His soul had left to be with the Lord. I wanted my last memory of him to be of our special day and how I had held and loved him. Additionally, I'll always treasure the memory of how he loved me when he expressed himself through his eyes. He died at seven thirty in the evening of February 16, 2014. I will remember that day as long as I live. Our last day spent on earth together was incredibly peaceful and special. It was a gift before his departure.

I thanked God first and foremost for the strength and courage to face that day. I felt God's presence through His unconditional love throughout the day. **His promise of His presence**, that "He shall never leave me nor abandon me," was an anchor during the most difficult loss of my adult life.

I had never been through any experience like that. It felt surreal, like a dream. I believe that a part of me had been severed or numbed out (as I call it). While I was waiting in the family room of the hospice, the nurse brought me Mike's ring, which had been his father's, and his watch.

I proceeded to go through the surreal motions of handling his death. First I called my mother, who had been my rock throughout the whole experience. She felt terrible that I had experienced Mike's death alone, with none of my family there for me. She lived in Pennsylvania and couldn't physically be there for me. "Don't worry, Mom," I said. "God is with me every step of the way. For you see, I'm not really alone."

I called Mike's cousin Melanie, then Lefty, my manager at work, and my sister, and the list went on and on. The intensity of the moment overwhelmed me as I sat in the oversized club chair by myself. I had to press forward. Although I had been blessed with great health and never experienced headaches before, my head ached like it was in a compressor. My heart ached with sadness that words cannot describe.

Next, an "angel of light," the compassionate nurse who had brought me Mike's belongings, appeared with a list of crematories in the local area. I had only three hours to decide where his body would go. If I did not decide within that time frame, his body would go to the county morgue. There was no way that would happen. However, I thought to myself, *How can I focus on making a decision during the intensity of emotions surrounding me?*

Thankfully, the nurse suggested two crematories that were dignified and affordable with good reputations. She guided me through a difficult, dark night, a light that I needed at the time. I thanked God for sending her at the right time. I chose a crematory that she suggested. I felt a sense of protection over Mike as I watched his covered body go to the elevator with the undertaker. I then collected his belongings, his suitcase, and his clothes. I gave Mike's roses to the nurse with gratitude as I thanked her and said goodbye. I drove home completely numb with profound sadness. My heart was broken. I had lost my other half.

I understand what it means to be a "survivor"; a part of me died when Mike died. When the doctor told Mike his life was nearing its end before being transferred to hospice, Mike gave up the fight, the will to live. He surrendered to the peace of death four days later. As angry as I was at the doctor for saying those debilitating words that diminished Mike's hope, I knew that Mike no longer wanted to be on earth. He sincerely desired to be at peace with the Lord in heaven.

When he drank during his last year of life, he said repeatedly, "I wish I was lucky enough to be in heaven, but I'm not that lucky." Mike carried more pain in his young body of forty-four years than any other man I had ever known. He felt life and losses deeply. His tender heart also loved deeply. He had never recovered after losing his father six years earlier—the father he loved and admired. Additionally, even with my many attempts at intervention through addiction recovery programs and grieving specialists, Mike never recovered after losing his older brother, Peter, to suicide fourteen months earlier. Mike chose not to heal. In the end, he ultimately got what he desired in that he didn't want to be here anymore. He was free from the intense pain that he had carried throughout his life.

It has been my experience that addicts have the largest hearts in that they feel life more deeply. This was certainly the case with Mike. It is my hope and intention that we look past the label of "alcoholic" or "addict" to look more deeply at who the person really is. We humans are too quick to judge, too quick to identify through "labels." If I had looked only at the label when I first met Mike, I would have missed God's gift that was placed into my life. I had never known any human being who evenly remotely possessed the pure heart that Mike had.

Michael's wishes were for me to scatter his ashes in Hawaii, but his mother chose not to honor those wishes. She made the decision to keep his ashes in the same way she kept Peter's ashes for herself.

By law, Mike's mother was next of kin, and it was her right and prerogative to receive Mike's ashes. I had no choice but to accept her decision. If Mike's ashes gave her comfort, then I'm sure he would be happy with that decision. However, I do believe in abiding by your loved one's dying wishes.

Even though I was without Mike's ashes, I pressed forward two weeks later with an informal funeral for Mike's closest friends. I planned the funeral on our special beach at sunset. I have many wonderful memories that I cherish of our walks and time spent at Deerfield Beach, particularly the tropical-style restaurant overlooking the ocean.

My sister, whom I had forgiven, showed her support and love as she attended the funeral and dinner. Through God's help of unlocking the door toward forgiveness to my sister, her presence was appreciated and a step toward healing. My boss, whose home I managed, was very thoughtful and generous in paying for the funeral and dinner. He also called regularly to make sure I was okay. Scott, my coworker and friend, was also helpful to me. His guidance and advice with decision making about the details surrounding Mike's death and funeral was invaluable to me. Our daily conversations were of great comfort.

Scott also offered to prepare the open funeral space by taking chairs over if necessary. We never needed chairs, though, as we stood to honor Mike during the funeral service. I had received permission from the town of Deerfield Beach to use a public balcony overlooking the ocean for Mike's funeral. A Christian minister from hospice drove from Palm Beach Gardens to lead the service. I gave the eulogy and spoke words from my heart. I spoke about Mike's extraordinary heart, particularly his kindness and generosity toward others.

After the funeral, I took my guests across the street to where we had an amazing dinner in honor and remembrance of Mike. We shared our memories of him. I brought pictures of Mike that I had passed around to my guests. It was a pleasant surprise that we were seated at the exact table in the restaurant where Mike's and my special spot was, overlooking the ocean.

I have no knowledge of whether Michael's family ever had a funeral for him. I never had any contact with Mike's mother after he passed away, because Mike's phone had been shut off for nonpayment. I had informed Melanie of his death, and she had proceeded to inform Mike's mother of the news. The news had to be devastating to her after having lost her eldest son, Peter, only fourteen months earlier. She had a friend with whom she worked call me for the details about Michael's death. She herself never called me. I wrote her a letter and placed the key to Peter's home in the envelope with it.

Michael hadn't wanted his mother to know that he was near death because he had no relationship with her. It placed me in an awkward situation in handling his final weeks and days on earth. I did my best to abide by his dying wishes.

I also attended a special memorial service that the hospice later provided at a local country club, honoring Michael as well as others who had passed away. Since Miriam was unable to attend the funeral that I had invited Mike's friends to partake in, she accompanied me to the memorial service. Her warmth was a comfort to me.

Hospice of Palm Beach County not only provided excellent comfort to Mike in his final days, but offered care beyond the death in terms of free grief therapy and the memorial service. I entered their private grief therapy program for a year, determined to heal. I was placed in the care of counselor Jean Godfrey. I will always be grateful for her valuable insight and counseling during the most painful time of my adult life. Their level of care was greatly appreciated and shall never be forgotten.

Before Mike's death, as difficult as life was from the abandonment I experienced when I first moved to Florida and then Mike's mental and physical deterioration, I had learned that it was possible to live above my circumstances in joy and peace through Christ. I wouldn't have seen God's great power if it hadn't been for my difficulties.

The best decision I have ever made was the moment I gave my heart to Christ. I came to that decision in my late thirties. I was in spiritual infancy at the time, but God grew me step by step through trials and hardships. As I grew in my relationship with the Lord daily, I learned that His power and strength was the key to my peace and fulfillment during Michael's final days. "The joy of the Lord is my strength" (Nehemiah 8:10).

We have the power of the spirit to overcome any obstacles when we apply His Word to our lives. The Enemy doesn't want us to know we have power in Christ. The Enemy lies and distorts with the saying, "Followers of Christ are for weak people." Guard against making the mistake of believing that lie. Deception is in full force these days. God has a purpose and a plan to empower us to reach and fulfill our destiny.

In all of my hardship and suffering that I had endured, I was anchored in God's presence, love, and peace. "But those who wait on the Lord shall renew their strength; they shall mount up with wings like eagles, they shall run and not be weary, they shall walk and not faint" (Isaiah 40:31).

For every trial and heartache, God is sufficient no matter what the circumstances. We can count on God's promises and build our lives on them, for He always does what He says. God had seen me through every hardship, never leaving nor abandoning me when imperfect human relationships failed. **God promises His presence and comfort** through all pain and suffering through His Word. "This is my comfort in my affliction, for Your Word has given me life" (Psalm 119:50).

I once asked myself, *What is the purpose for our pain and suffering?* I have discovered three answers. First, it is through our suffering that we grow and mature to be more compassionate human beings. Pain produces growth. We learn our greatest lessons through hardship. Second, God permits pain and suffering to draw us closer to Him in relationship. Third, we may never have all the answers to know why God allows certain hardships to happen, but we know that we can *trust* God to carry us in the palm of His hand during our darkest storms.

God brings us through the fire to become stronger, and more polished and loving than before. If we trust in Him, He promises that our ashes shall be turned into beauty. Dr. Charles Stanley explains eloquently that "In this way, our suffering is not wasted, but actually becomes our blessings. God intends for us to profit from our hardships."

Life is tremendously harder when we try to fix problems on our own. Life is incredibly lighter when we let God carry our burdens and trials. Every trial has an expiration date. God's Word has not only revived me, but given me a new hope and outlook. My hope has been renewed as I walk in the newness of life. I may not know exactly the details of my future, for it is unknown, but I know and believe with all my heart that God's unconditional love will provide every need along my path as illustrated through my "love story."

Jesus' life is our evidence of God's unconditional love for us. God's nature is love. Jesus came to earth to bring us new life. I learned to love more deeply from the teachings of Jesus. I thank God for the gift of love and for teaching me how to love. Michael was placed into my life to love me and for me to love him in return.

God's Word is a road map providing promises and directions to meet every challenge and heartache we will ever face. God's Word stands forever. "The grass withers, the flower fades, but the Word of our God stands forever" (Isaiah 40:8).

Mike's pure heart endlessly helped others in that he put others' needs before his own. He has inspired me in ways I haven't even fully recognized yet. In the end, Michael cared for everyone, but he didn't know how to care for himself.

Death will not have the last word, for he who believes has eternal life. I know that Mike is home, out of pain, and in God's love and peace. I'll never know what could have been, but I know that I am forever changed for the better through having known and loved Michael. For as long as I live, Mike too will live, for he is now a part of me forever.

> *There are some who bring a light so great to the world that even after they have gone, the light remains.*
> —*Unknown*

It is my prayer that those who suffer with addictions will press into God for divine power and deliverance.

Prayer for Addiction: "Father God, I need your help to overcome my addiction. I believe in faith that you are removing this addiction from my life. I ask in the name of Jesus that you set me free from this addiction. I pray for complete healing and transformation not just for myself, but so that others would be blessed by my testimony. Your Word promises: You will never leave me nor forsake me in that You love me unconditionally. I claim the victory to overcome this addiction in Jesus' name. Amen."

# God's Seven Promises Fulfilled

Promise #1:  His Presence

"Be strong and of good courage, do not fear nor be afraid of them; for the Lord your God, He is the One who goes with you. He will not leave you nor forsake you" (Deuteronomy 31:6).

Promise #2:  His Protection

"As for God, His way is perfect; the word of the Lord is proven; He is a shield to all who trust in Him. For who is God, except the Lord? And who is a rock, except our God? God is my strength and power, and He makes my way perfect" (2 Samuel 22:31–33).

Promise #3:  His Forgiveness

"Condemn not, and you shall not be condemned. Forgive, and you will be forgiven" (Luke 6:37).

## Promise #4:  His Blessing (to those who wait upon the Lord)

"Therefore the Lord will wait, that He may be gracious to you; And therefore He will be exalted, that He may have mercy on you. For the Lord is a God of justice; blessed are all those who wait for Him" (Isaiah 30:18).

## Promise #5:  His Comfort

"Who comforts us in all our tribulation, that we may be able to comfort those who are in any trouble, with the comfort with which we ourselves are comforted by God" (2 Corinthians 1:4).

## Promise #6:  His Strength

"I can do all things through Christ who strengthens me" (Philippians 4:13).

## Promise #7:  His Love

"And we have known and believed the love that God has for us. God is love, and he who abides in love abides in God, and God in him" (1 John 4:16).

# About the Author

Karen Sacchetti, a creative dance educator, author, and creator of Adagio Stretch, pursued her education at both Pennsylvania State University and Lesley University in Cambridge, Massachusetts, earning her bachelor of arts degree in drama, dance, and education from the latter in 1998. Karen established Adagio Stretch, www.karensacchetti.com. Designing her own unique program for adults, she implements the foundations of dance through a therapeutic approach to optimize brain and body functioning. In the early to mid-1990s, Karen acted and danced at the Riverside Theater in Boston. She later performed as an actress, singer, and dancer for the South County Center for the Arts in Rhode Island. Karen is committed to Christ Fellowship, her church home and has been endorsed by the Marquis Who's Who® as a leader in education, health, and wellness. Karen received the Albert Nelson Marquis Lifetime Achievement Award and is a resident of Boca Raton, Florida.

9 781545 645420